OPEN ROAD'S

New York City
with Kids!

Laurie Bain Wilson

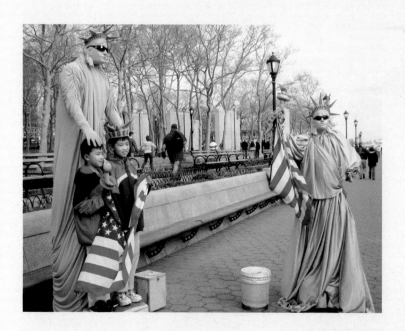

Open Road Family Travel Guides – designed to give
you the *best* choices for your family vacation!

Open Road Publishing

Open Road's new travel guides.
Designed to cut to the chase.
You don't need a huge travel encyclopedia – you need a *selective guide* to
steer you right. If you're going on vacation for a few weeks or less, get a
guide that brings you the *best* of any destination!

Open Road – the guide you need for the trip you want.

The New Open Road Travel Guides.
Right to the point.
Uncluttered.
Easy.

*To my most amazing son Alexander, or AWIL, always keep you head high
and your glove down.*

Open Road Publishing
P.O. Box 284, Cold Spring Harbor, NY 11724
www.openroadguides.com

Text Copyright©2008 by Laurie Bain Wilson
- All Rights Reserved -
ISBN 13: 978-159360-110-7
ISBN 10: 159360-110-2
Library of Congress Control No. 2008922623

About the Author

Laurie Bain Wilson is a travel writer whose specialty is family travel. Her other books
include *The Unofficial Guide to New England and New York with Kids* and *Open
Road's New York City Made Easy*. She is a contributing author to *How To Organize
Just About Everything*. Laurie lives in Sea Cliff, New York, with her son Alexander.

The author has made every effort to be as accurate as possible, but neither she nor the
publisher assumes responsibility for the services provided by any business listed in this
guide; for any errors or omissions; or any loss, damage, or disruptions in your travels
for any reason.

For photo credits turn to page 206.

CONTENTS

(continued)

Maps

Acknowledgments

A special thanks to Jackie Bain, my beautiful mother, who is from Boston but roots for the Yankees, as well as for me and Alex; to Donald Bain, my handsome father, who has helped me so much; to my great-grandfather, Major League catcher Con Daily, (thanks for cheering for Alex); to Donna Kuper, my oldest, dearest, forever friend and is always there for us; to my sister Pamela Bain Shippee and nephews Zach, Luke and Jake; to Colleen Brewer and Cheryl Coutts, you are heros and I miss you; to awesome 12-year-old Morgan Coutts, the strongest girl I've ever met; to my cousins Janet and Jill Pearl and Tommy, John and Gino Sullivan—thanks for the fun memories (I miss you); to my goddaughter Kirsten Peterson, (I think of you a lot); to Debbie Tuma, Rebecca Brubaker Roberts, Karen Carraro, Steven Raff and Phil Maffa for friendship when I needed it most; to Helen Senesky, thanks for being so patient and so kind to Alex through the years; to all of the 9/11 Cantor Fitzgerald families whose faces I will never forget; many thanks to my editor and publisher Jonathan Stein for his unwavering support and kindness, as well as his enthusiasm for New York's family-friendly treasures; and finally, to New Yorkers, who are simply the best.

1. INTRODUCTION

My son Alexander was born in New York City, a town millions of children proudly call home. These kids love to share their backyard (Central Park), their playgrounds, their restaurants, their favorite museums and their passion for New York. They make sure the Big Apple doesn't lose its youthful charm, despite being the most sophisticated and cosmopolitan of cities.

And that plan to kill New York's soul, to rip out its heart and to destroy its reputation as the world's most sensational city: *Fuhgedaboudit!* September 11 personified New York, and New Yorkers—of every age—have become fiercely defensive of their city while also extremely generous in showing visitors a good time. Tourists, too, are in awe of this great town and have come out in force; in 2007, New York City welcomed a record 46-million tourists. Talk about strength in numbers! And, New York was recently ranked one of the top five places that parents had on their wish list to vacation with their children.

Even the brattiest of New Yorkers stroll wide-and-starry-eyed at the city's wonders. And every morning brings the promise of a new discovery, a new treat for the senses, a gift. The city's spirit is as contagious as a deep belly laugh—you'll catch it and pass it along. Promise. Yes, you'll find some crab apples and worms in the Big Apple. But, when you pack up to return home, you'll agree that New York is one helluva town.

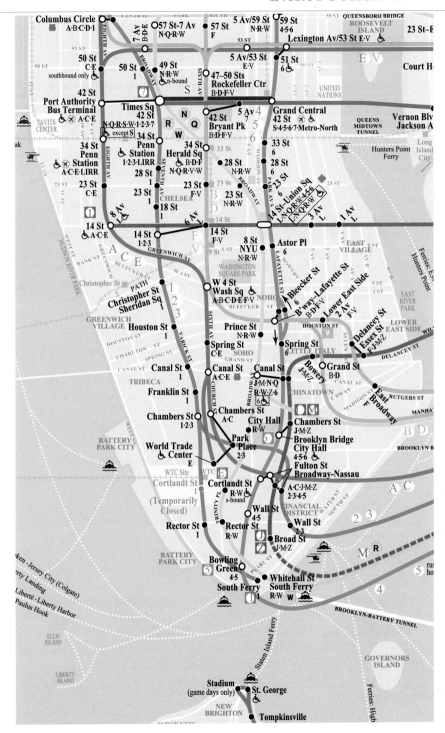

2. OVERVIEW

As a travel editor and writer for my entire professional career, I have traveled to many wonderful distant spots around the world. When my son was born, I packed him along for journeys. We snorkeled in the Turks and Caicos, kayaked the still waters off Prince Edward Island, tracked down Mickey at Walt Disney World, fired up the barbecue on Cape Cod beaches, relived history at the Cooperstown Baseball Hall of Fame, hiked Vermont, and munched on the sweetest pineapple in Hawaii.

Yet, no matter how exciting or fabulous our trips are, when our plane flies over Manhattan to bring us home or our car crosses one of the bridges, I always get a rush. And, yet, I see magical Manhattan all the time. I can only imagine the thrill of experiencing it as a visitor.

From a distance, the City's skyline is a tease. Experience its neighborhoods and its people and New York flirts even more with incredible restaurants, enthralling attractions, mind-boggling museums and welcoming hotels. New York's reputation as a cultural mecca is undeniable. From Broadway shows to Carnegie Hall concerts to Lincoln Center performances to the Metropolitan Museum of Art's exhibits, Manhattan is a canvas for the arts. Kudos, too, to New York for being named the "Sporting Capital of the United States" – home to the Knicks, Yankees, Mets, Rangers, U.S. Open Tennis and the New York City Marathon, to name just a few of the great sports teams and events.

TRAVEL TIPS

A successful vacation in the City takes careful planning—but the plan should be flexible. That's the New York way. Have a plan—but remember things change here in a New York minute (that's the beauty of the City, really.) As parents, you know full well the importance of being able to go with the flow.

It's necessary also to build in extra time to get where you want to get. Traffic in New York can come to a crawl for any number of reasons—and often does. If you have theater tickets for an 8 o'clock show, build in lots of getting-there time. Word to the wise: If you're not sure, ask. New Yorkers are very friendly and love to give directions. They're fast talkers so pay attention, but they'll get you there the quickest way.

To ensure a successful family trip, keep the following pointers in mind:

Build in lots of down time. That can mean hanging out at Central Park, at one of the City's playgrounds or at the hotel swimming pool. Wherever you choose to decom-

press, make sure you do it. New York is a vital town—you'll eventually feed off its energy (and so will your kids) and you won't want to miss a beat. My son is always on the go, hates to be bored and I attribute this to living in the City. Your kids, too, will love all the excitement and want to keep going and going and going. But they'll burn out if you're not careful.

Make the trip as interactive as possible. Many kids love to have a map of wherever they are in their travels. You can pick up free maps at many places throughout the City, as well as subway maps, which kids also love. Also, encourage them to keep a journal of their days and nights in the Big Apple.

Part of the fun in New York is walking the streets. My son and I often choose to walk rather than ride, no matter the distance. However, most kids who are visiting *love* riding the subways—to them it's an attraction, not a way of getting around.

Get them involved in planning the days' itineraries. "Should we take the bus or subway?" "Do you think we should walk down East 45th Street or East 46th Street?"

Establish some routines. For example, give each child $20 a day to spend; they can save it up to buy one thing at the end of the trip or buy something every day. Also, with younger children, don't skip meals—make sure they know there's breakfast, lunch and dinner every day, just like at home.

Try to avoid befuddled expectations. Many kids are old enough and have traveled enough to establish reference points, but still have gaping voids in their mental pictures of their world. For example, when my son was young, he feared that the waffles he was served for breakfast at one of the authentic taverns at historic Colonial Williamsburg were also "old;" imagined that our car would tumble off one of Cape Breton's especially curvaceous roads in Nova Scotia; and expected to be able to pet the whales while on a whale-watching excursion off Cape Cod. Anticipate and listen to what's going on in their minds.

Teens love headphones, and they certainly can come in handy in keeping the peace. However, walking the streets of any city with music piped into your ears isn't the best idea in the world. New York is a town where you need to be alert (part of its allure, anyway, are the sounds of honking taxis, spirited conversations and street musicians).

Art museums can be enjoyable if kids have some background information about what they are seeing. Most of the museums in the City have family guides or exhibit-related games and puzzles. Make sure to ask when you arrive at the museum.

A vacation for single parents and kids is an oxymoron. New York is filled with tons of single parents and their kids so you won't feel alone. However, you most likely won't get any down time, either. Think about inviting a close friend or relative (or, more importantly, close friends of your children). This might be prohibitive because of the cost (hotel rooms in Manhattan tend to be small and there might not be enough room), but if you can, the trip might be more enjoyable. Unlike resort destinations, New York City is not the type of getaway where your child can hang out at a children's program while you sightsee or read a book on the beach. For older teens, you might consider investing in walkie-talkies or a cell phone so you can give them at least a little space—and for peace of mind in the event you get separated.

NEW YORK CITY NEIGHBORHOODS

I've prepared some brief sketches of each major neighborhood that will help you plan your trip:

Lower Manhattan

Unfortunately, the southernmost tip of Manhattan is etched in most of the world's memory as the tragic spot where the devastating act of terrorism hit on 9/11. Many tourists to this part of town come to view the World Trade Center site and to pay their respects to the heroes who lost their lives here. Make no mistake about it though, lower Manhattan is still the financial center of the world: The New York Stock Exchange is here, as is the Federal Reserve Bank. And it's also home to South Street Seaport and Battery Park City.

Little Italy/NoLita/Chinatown

Little Italy isn't the same as when I lived on nearby Sullivan Street in

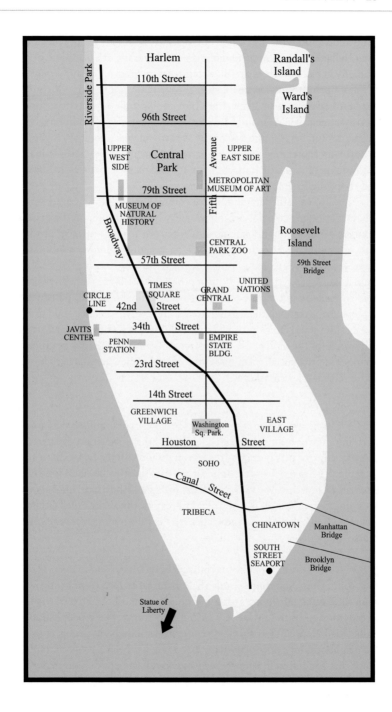

Soho and would walk the couple of blocks to Little Italy for my pick of a great Italian meal at a lively neighborhood restaurant. It's lost some of its ethnicity in recent years as a result of residents moving out to say *bon giorno* to the suburbs (think *Sopranos*). But it's still a fun spot to visit. Of course the best reason to visit Little Italy (not unlike Italy itself) is the food. Narrow streets like Mott and Mulberry are flanked with a handful of good Italian restaurants, though not nearly as many in year's gone by. If you're in town in September you're in for an Italian treat: the San Gennaro Festival takes over Little Italy with sausage and peppers, zepoles, cannolis, and festive lights and music.

Chinatown is the largest Chinese community in the Western Hemisphere, a vibrant, colorful neighborhood with lots of buzz and activity. Tourists—and New Yorkers—love Chinatown for a great meal of dim sum. Chinatown is also the spot to snag a street bargain. My son's older sister, Jessica, loves to scour Chinatown's streets for handbag knockoffs. Chinatown is also tons of fun during the Chinese New Year. Fireworks used to explode but have been banned in recent years. Still, parades of dragons snake through the narrow streets, and everybody has a good time.

NoLita stands for North of Little Italy, and it's where you can stroll and search for the kind of off-beat merchandise you won't find in upscale boutiques uptown such as unique embroidered purses, hand-crafted boots and interesting jewelry pieces.

Lower East Side

While the rest of Manhattan moves in a New York minute, the Lower East Side moves a bit slower. In the 1800's, the Lower East Side was a gateway slum for new immigrants and you should visit the Lower East Side Tenement Museum to get a taste of what it used to be like. This is a fascinating museum for kids. Orchard Street is a hot spot for bargain shopping. There is also a handful of ethnic eateries like Katz's Delicatessen where stacked corned beef sandwiches are the rule, and pickles and knish spots.

Soho/Noho/Tribeca/Greenwich Village/East Village

Soho (which stands for South of Houston Street) has come a long way from the days of loft-living artists and quiet neighborhood streets, thanks to the infusion of trendy boutiques and restaurants. Some people, especially jaded New Yorkers think it's come *too* far along—at the expense of the neighborhood's once artsy flair. Yes, there has been a proliferation of shops that you'd find in Anywhere U.S.A. But having once lived in Soho,

I can tell you that this is still very much a neighborhood with mom and pop shops like Joe's Dairy on Sullivan Street. Joe's makes and sells the best mozzarella anywhere in the City. Stop in and get some fresh out of the oven. The art scene is still very much alive in Soho, with an estimated 250 art galleries alone. The moral of this tale is that if you seek you shall find the fabric of Soho of days past.

NoHo (which stands for North of Houston Street) is a relatively new neighborhood with some trendy restaurants and stores. And Tribeca, which stands for Triangle Below Canal Street, is home to a handful of hip restaurants, cool shops and loft apartments (John F. Kennedy Jr. and Carolyn Bissette lived here). However, NoHo and Tribeca don't have near the number of shops and restaurants and tourists that Soho does.

Greenwich Village has always been a bohemian mix of unique shops, cafes, bookstores, jazz clubs, off-off Broadway theaters and it still is. Teens especially love to spend time down here (think body piercing, dyed hair, spiked hair, grunge jeans and you've got the makings for a teen dream-come-true.) Washington Square Park is a lively concrete-and-grassy-square that's popular with nearby NYU students—there's always something or someone interesting to see.

The East Village has a rep as a really far out, progressive neighborhood. It probably isn't the spot for a Sunday brunch with grandma (unless your last name is Osbourne), but your 15 year old will think it's totally bad (that's a good thing.) Rebellious teens especially love this part of the City with its salty edge—in fact, it makes Greenwich Village look like Parochial school.

Flatiron District

Named for the really interesting-shaped, brick-and-limestone Flatiron Building at 23rd St. and Broadway (you'll know it when you see it, it's the building that's shaped like an iron), this area is architecturally stunning. The Flatiron District is home to one of the City's best playgrounds and kid-friendly parks, Madison Square Park. And Union Square, home to the popular Greenmarket, where New Yorkers buy fresh, farm produce, is also here.

Gramercy Park

A chic, tree-lined residential neighborhood with a gated (key, please) park. There are a couple of great restaurants and shops in the Gramercy Park neighborhood, but it's primarily a residential part of town.

Murray Hill

Another residential section of the City with little else going on—and the people who live here wouldn't want it any other way. (Technically, the Empire State Building is in Murray Hill, but it's really more of a midtown location).

Chelsea

Not too long ago, Chelsea was an invisible neighborhood, with not much to offer in the way of culture, dining or nightlife. It's on the map now, thanks in part to the sprawling and ambitious Chelsea Piers Sports Complex and the many art galleries, cafés and boutiques. It's also home to the city's gay population, who moved uptown from the Village.

Clinton

Just to the north of Chelsea, this neighborhood was once known as Hell's Kitchen (translation: porn shops, condemned apartments). It's been cleaned up, "renamed" and, while still not the most desirable of addresses in town, it's come a long way.

Theater District/Times Square

This celebrated New York neighborhood, once seedy and scary, now is one of the city's most popular tourist spots—for kids! Toy's 'R Us opened an enormous store here, complete with indoor Ferris wheel. A handful of

hotels and restaurants (ESPN Zone scores big) have super transformed Times Square with more neon, blinking lights and action than ever. Times Square is where it's at.

Midtown

Skyscraper office buildings, chic restaurants and city landmarks are what this part of town is all about. During the holidays, midtown is packed with tourists who stroll Fifth Avenue to admire the holiday displays and the illustrious tree at Rockefeller Center. Midtown is also where you'll find the highest concentration of hotels (although Times

Square is catching up), Grand Central Station and, to the east, the United Nations.

Upper East Side

Manhattan's most upscale and expensive neighborhood is where you'll discover an impressive collection of museums, boutiques, trendy restaurants, and elegant townhouse mansions, especially along lovely Madison Avenue.

Stroll this neighborhood on a weekday morning or afternoon and you'll see lots of nannies pushing Cadillac strollers and socialites dining on *foie gras* at outdoor cafes. The Upper East Side is noticeably quieter than the Upper West—there's not as much traffic and less horn honking (relatively speaking).

Note: There is no subway that runs from the Upper East to the Upper West sides; Central Park divides the two. Your best bet: Take the cross-town bus at 79th or 86th streets, or walk across the Park.

Central Park

The heart and soul of New York City, Central Park is a breath of fresh air—literally and figuratively speaking. It's an 843-acre backyard for New Yorkers who dwell in small, cramped apartments. They come to bike, jog, stroll, walk their dogs, have a picnic, listen to outdoor concerts, blow off steam…Central Park also tugs at the hearts of tourists with scenic skyline views, rambling paths, grassy lawns and, that famous restaurant, Tavern on the Green.

Upper West Side

Manhattan's Upper West is funkier and artier than the Upper East. While stockbrokers and real estate moguls tend to live on the Upper East, writers, editors, dancers, actors and musicians opt for the Upper West. The American Museum of Natural History is a magnet for families—this is the most popular museum for kids in the city. You'll also discover Lincoln Center, the largest cultural complex in the world, and the swanky Time Warner Center in this part of town.

Morningside Heights

The neighborhood above Central Park (to the west) lies this busy part of town, home to Columbia University, the Cathedral of St. John the Divine (the Blessings of the Animals service is not to be missed) and Riverside Church, another glorious landmark.

Harlem/Washington Heights

Once down and out, Harlem is on the map as a hip place to be. The neighborhood has a jazzy past (jazz artists like Count Bassie, Duke Ellington and Dizzy Gillepsie used to play in clubs here), and it's still the place to hear great music from gospel to jazz. Bill Clinton made news when he chose to rent office space here. Also, a number of popular, trendy stores have opened in Harlem. But in the midst of the gentrification, Harlem has retained its soul and spirituality. Travel way north to Washington Heights and you'll come to The Cloisters in Fort Tyron Park with pretty views of the Hudson and great medieval art.

The Bronx

While the Bronx Bombers might think the curse of Babe Ruth is one theory for the Yankees success, residents up here think it's the Bronx that's the lucky charm. Yankee Stadium is one great reason to visit the Bronx. But there are others, like the Bronx Zoo and the New York Botanical Garden.

Queens

Queens is extremely ethnically diverse, with pockets of Indian, Jamaican, Greek, Chinese, Korean and other neighborhoods rich in ethnicity scattered throughout.

Staten Island

Really closer to New Jersey than the City, Staten Island is home to many commuters who make the daily ride on the Staten Island ferry into lower Manhattan. There are a handful of attractions (Staten Island Children's Museum and Staten Island Zoo). Not many tourists visit Staten Island though—but a free ride on the Staten Island Ferry is tourist must-do.

Brooklyn

Brooklyn is one of my favorite neighborhoods, and has been a favorite spot of writers for decades (Walt Whitman and Arthur Miller lived here). There are also tremendous views of downtown Manhattan from the Brooklyn Promenade. And DUMBO (Down Under the Manhattan Bridge Overpass) has given Brooklyn a new edge with artsy events and trendy eateries. All said, Brooklyn is Manhattan—centuries ago. Used to be that people who worked in Manhattan opted to live in Brooklyn, thanks to cheaper rents. Not anymore. Finding an affordable apartment in the nice sections of Brooklyn (Brooklyn Heights, Cobble Hill, Park Slope) is no less competitive than trying to secure one across the bridge in the big city.

When visiting Manhattan, do make the time to walk across the Brooklyn Bridge—a stunning, one-mile long suspension bridge that took almost two decades to build. A tourist must-do.

KIDS' ITINERARY
Day One
Morning

Enjoy breakfast at one of the city's diners.

If kids are old enough (see information under Lower Manhattan chapter), head way downtown to Lower Manhattan to visit St. Paul's Chapel and Ground Zero. Then, take the ferry and visit Ellis Island and the Statue of Liberty. Note: You can also opt to visit just Ellis Island or just the Statue of Liberty (the ferry stops first at the Statue and then onto Ellis). You can buy advanced tickets by calling 877/LADYTIX. (For more information, see info under Ellis Island and Statue of Liberty entry.)

If you're not up for visiting the Statue of Liberty or Ellis Island but would like to see the Statue, board the Staten Island ferry for a ride that will afford great views of Lady Liberty. The best part: the ferry is free roundtrip.

Afternoon

If you do visit Ellis Island or the Statue of Liberty, you can purchase lunch at either spot (or, pick up sandwiches in town to bring with you). Otherwise, when you disembark the ferry in lower Manhattan, make your way up to Soho and the Village and lunch at one of the restaurants we've listed in that section (Balthazar in Soho is a great spot). After lunch, stroll the streets of Soho and the Village and perhaps also take in Little Italy and the East Village. Then, it's naptime/rest back at the hotel. Or, if your hotel has a pool, take a swim.

Evening

Have dinner at one of the family-friendly restaurants in Times Square (see listings). Or, dine at a more upscale affair like the Oyster Bar in Grand Central Station.

Take in a Broadway or off-Broadway show or an IMAX movie.

Day Two
Morning

Rise and shine and grab breakfast at a diner or bagel shop.

If it's a lovely day, go to the Central Park Zoo. If not, spend the morning at the American Museum of Natural History—or, if your children love art, opt for the Metropolitan Museum of Art, Museum of Modern Art, the Guggenheim Museum or the Whitney Museum of Art.

Afternoon

Lunch at one of the museums. Or, head to Central Park to dine at the Boathouse restaurant.

If you're up for it, rent a rowboat and take an easy row on the lake after lunch. Otherwise, stroll over to the Zoo (if you didn't hit it in the morning) or take a spin on the Carousel.

For lunch, you might opt to go downtown instead to Madison Square Park for burgers and shakes at the Shake Shack.

Take tea at the Plaza Hotel or the Waldorf Astoria.

Then, back to the hotel for rest and/or a swim.

Evening

Early dinner in the garden at Tavern on the Green (seasonal). Then check out one of the kid-friendly and inexpensive performances at Tada or New Victory Theater. Or if you're traveling with young girls go to the American Girl Place for a show and something to eat.

A visit to the top of the Empire State Building (closes at midnight).

TEENAGERS' ITINERARY

Okay, first off, there's a huge difference between traveling with a teenage girl and a teenage boy. In a word: shopping. Your son could care less about shopping; your daughter could care less about anything else. And so, the following itineraries are skewed to please both genders.

Day One
Morning

Thanks to hormone overdrive, they'll want to sleep in. Remind them that they are in the City That Never Sleeps. Grab breakfast at a New York City diner. Then, take the subway to Brooklyn and walk across the Brooklyn Bridge to Manhattan (or, if you're up for it, take the subway to South Street Seaport, grab breakfast there, then walk across the Brooklyn Bridge *and back.)*

Visit St. Paul's Chapel and the World Trade Center site

Board ferry for Statue of Liberty/Ellis Island. Or, if you're not interested in visiting either but would like to see the Statue of Liberty, hop aboard the Staten Island ferry and take the free roundtrip ride that gives you a nice view of Lady Liberty.

Afternoon

If you've decided to go to Ellis Island, you can buy and eat lunch there. Otherwise, make your way up to the Lower East Side to stroll Orchard, Grand and Delancey streets—chock-full of bargain shops and a buzz of activity. Chinatown is spot-on for dim sum lunch. Tour the Lower East Side Tenement Museum on Orchard Street.

Evening

Dinner at family-friendly Times Square restaurant (see listing). After dinner, see *Stomp, Blue Man Group* or off-Broadway shows that teens love.

If you've got the pizzazz, top off the evening at the city's only revolving rooftop restaurant and lounge, The View Restaurant and Lounge in the Marriott Marquis located in Times Square. Or, visit Top of the Rock at Rockefeller Center and take in the night views of Manhattan.

Day Two

Morning

They'll want to sleep in but tell them they can check their email at CyberCafé in Times Square (250 West 49th Street) while munching on oatmeal, bagels or eggs and that should help. If you're the lucky parent of a kid who could care less about the Internet, you have several options. If it's a nice day and your hotel is near Central Park or one of the City's other grassy spots, do like a New Yorker—grab a couple of bagels with cream cheese and the New York *Times* and enjoy a picnic breakfast. Or, opt to eat at one of the many diners around town or bagel shops.

Then, head for Times Square. Visit the Madame Tussaud Wax Museum. Later, stroll Times Square enjoying the street performers and neon scene. Teenage daughter tip: Stroll Fifth Avenue, window shopping along the way in the fabulous shops like Bendels, Tiffany & Co., Cartier, Saks Fifth Avenue and Cartier. On the other end of the cash flow spectrum, there's a gigantic H & M. Begin your outing at Rockefeller Center and St. Patrick's Cathedral across the street and walk uptown. You'll eventually come to 59th Street, flanked by the newly-renovated Plaza Hotel and FAO Schwarz, with Central Park a chestnut throw away. If your daughter insists on visiting Bloomingdales, walk east to Lexington Avenue. (You could visit the newer Bloomies in Soho later in the trip). Teenage son tip: He might also enjoy strolling Fifth Avenue thanks to the incredible NBA Store and Niketown.

If your son or daughter is a jock or a sports fan, head to ESPN Zone for lunch. Let them loose in the games area before settling in for lunch at the restaurant. Or backpedal a couple of blocks to Ellen's Stardust Diner at 51st and Broadway.

Afternoon

Now that you've satiated—or at least whet—their appetites for the things *they* like to do it's time to hit a museum. The Museum of Natural History is a must. But the Met is also an incredibly rich experience.

Evening

If you're in town during baseball season, why not head to the ballpark for a game and dinner? You have two choices: Yankee Stadium or Shea Stadium. Both are accessible by subway; Yankee Stadium is also available by boat (see individual listings). Or, head uptown to Yankees Stadium just to take the really cool Stadium tour.

If you're in town when baseball isn't, get tickets to a Broadway show. Or, you might be able to get Knicks or Rangers tickets for games at Madison Square Garden.

For dinner, go to Little Italy (see *I'm Hungry!* chapter).

After dinner (if you aren't at the ballpark or a Broadway Show) go to the top of the Empire State Building to see the City lights (open until midnight). Or, take the subway uptown to the roof sculpture garden at the Met Museum for pretty city views (seasonal).

Day Three
Morning

Okay, let them sleep in a little bit today and then go for a late breakfast at Balthazar in Soho.

Afternoon

Hit fashionable Soho. Peek into galleries and boutiques.

Stroll up to Greenwich Village to hang out.

Parent Tips

My 17-year-old (Alex's) Picks
- ESPN Zone
- Broadway Show
- Mickey Mantle Restaurant
- The Chelsea Screamer boat ride
- Yankees game at Yankee Stadium
- Museum of Natural History
- IMAX movie

Alex's 21-year-old sister's (Elizabeth's) Picks
- Times Square for souvenirs like T-shirts
- A deli sandwich from a New York Deli
- A slice of New York pizza
- A Broadway Show
- Grand Central Station ("Be sure to look up at the constellation on the ceiling.")
- Central Park

For lunch, go to John's Pizza in the Village or BLT Burger in the Union Square neighborhood.

Next up: Teenage boys and girls who are sports enthusiasts will love Chelsea Piers, a gigantic sports complex (see listing). Take the Chelsea *Screamer* boat sightseeing tour around Manhattan.

Evening

Take the subway to Grand Central Station to check it out (rush hour is a good time to see all the action). Have dinner at the Oyster Bar in Grand Central or at Mickey Mantle's midtown restaurant, or head back to Times Square where there are tons of family-friendly theme restaurants that kids love.

Check out the listings in the local papers, etc. for a concert, dance performance or theater performance.

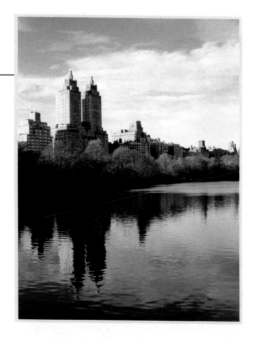

3. LOWER MANHATTAN, ELLIS ISLAND & THE BOWERY

Lower Manhattan is a heady mix of young stockbrokers in pinstripes (no, not the Yankees), seasoned politicians in partisan power suits and historic churches shadowed by soaring skyscrapers. This bustling part of the city, where the East and Hudson rivers meet, was also our nation's first capital. Unfortunately, this special part of Manhattan is now etched in most of the world's memory as the tragic spot where this country's most devastating act of terrorism hit on 9/11.

In addition to the financial center of the world—lower Manhattan is home to the New York Stock Exchange and Wall Street (originally a walled fortress built by Dutch setters in 1663)—it's also home to City Hall, where the city government is housed. There are other great things to do and see this far downtown, including visiting the Statue of Liberty on Ellis Island and The New Museum in the Bowery.

Strolling the streets in lower Manhattan is a humbling experience. During a weekend visit, you might stumble across a blockbuster movie shoot that attracts lots of excitement. Visit here on a weekday and the action begins when the bell rings at the Stock Exchange. Yet, while it may seem as business as usual, since 9/11 there is, and always will be, a tremendous void down here—quite figuratively, literally and spiritually—that will never in a million years be filled.

If your children are old enough—or, rather, are mature enough (it really doesn't matter how old they are biologically as each child's coping skills differs)—I recommend you begin your visit to New York City in lower Manhattan, specifically at St. Paul's Chapel and Ground Zero. It is a gentle reminder of the spirit and determination of this City, which you'll come to appreciate even more during your vacation here as you make your way uptown to explore all of the neighborhoods. Be prepared for your children to ask many questions and to revisit their feelings and emotions on that day. If they were old enough at the time, they'll forever remember where they were on 9/11 and a visit to the World Trade Center site will most likely cause them to revisit those memories.

Like millions of Americans on the morning of 9/11, I dropped my son off at school and got on a train to go into the city to work. As my train approached Manhattan I saw the burning towers. Cell phones rang in the

Touring Lower Manhattan

• Who says you have to have deep pockets on Wall Street? Take the free 90-minute walking tour, stopping off at Wall Street and the New York Stock Exchange (since 9/11 the Stock Exchange has been closed to visitors). Tours run every Thursday and Saturday beginning at noon. Meet at the front steps of the National Museum of the American Indian. Reservations aren't necessary. For more information, call Alliance for Downtown New York, 212/606-4064.

• Or, opt to take the self-guided Patriotic Trail (a better bet for families with young kids because you can stop at your leisure). This tour will take you about an hour (without stopping.) It begins one block east of the World Trade Center site at Broadway and Vesey Street and takes you to 19 sites that figured prominently in the birth of the nation. Pick up a brochure at NYC & Company's information kiosk in City Hall Park.

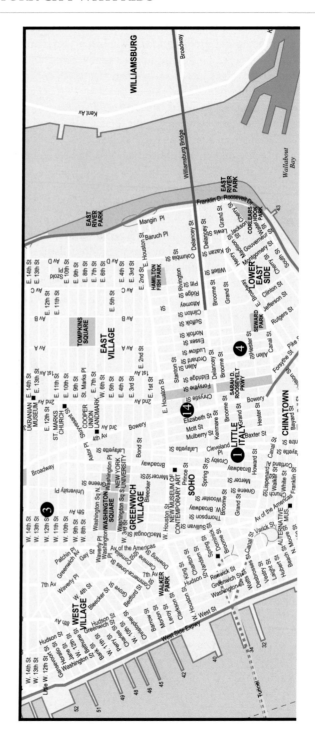

Lower Manhattan

1. Children's Museum of the Arts
2. Ellis Island/Statue of Liberty
3. Forbes Magazine Galleries
4. Lower East Side Tenement Museum
5. Museum of Jewish Heritage
6. Nat. Museum of the American Indian
7. National Sports Museum
8. New York City Police Museum
9. St. Paul's Chapel
10. Skyscraper Museum
11. South Street Seaport
12. Winter Garden Atrium/World Fin. Center
13. World Trade Center Site
14. The New Museum

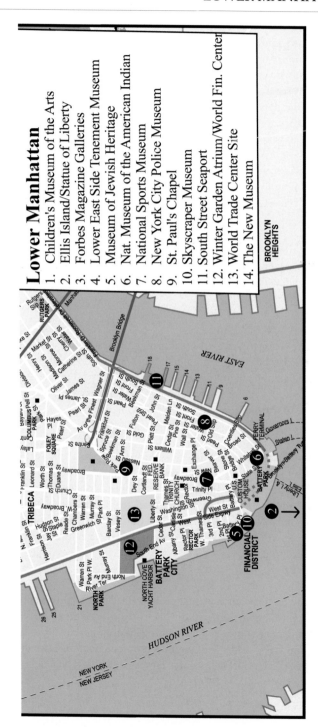

train car and word quickly spread among the commuters that the city was under attack. Some of my commuter friends had loved ones in the Towers. I also had friends who worked in the Towers. We watched in disbelief and confusion. I was separated from my son, ten years old at the time, and couldn't reach him because the phones were all out. Fighter jets flew over his school and they were not allowed outside at recess. He'd been told something had happened in Manhattan and he knew I was headed there to work that day.

My son just recently visited the World Trade Center site. It's a personal decision and one which parents should give some thought to beforehand. Of course, one day the site will be a memorial in some shape and form.

Federal Hall National Memorial

26 Wall Street (at Broad St.), Tel. 212/825-6888, www.nps.gov/feha.

Open: Monday through Friday 9am to 5pm. Closed Saturday, Sunday.

Admission: Free.

Subway: 2, 3, 4. 5, J, M, and Z.

This is where George Washington was inaugurated back in 1789. You can take a guided tour (or a self-guided tour) to see the Bible that Washington used at his inauguration and there are also several interactive exhibits. There's also a junior ranger program during which kids learn about the American Revolution and George Washington.

St. Paul's Chapel

Broadway (between Fulton and Vesey Streets, adjacent to World Trade Center site), Tel. 212/233-4264, www.saintpaulschapel.org.

Open: The Ground Zero Ministry Exhibit is open Monday through Saturday from 10am to 6pm and Sunday from 8am to 4pm; a concert series takes place on Mondays between 1pm and 2pm (during which the exhibit closes). There is also a Prayers for Peace worship service held daily between 12:30pm and 12:45pm.

Admission: Free.

Subway: 2, 3, 4. 5, 6, A, E, R.

For years, this darling church with its pretty stained glass windows and pews has had a special spot in the hearts of New Yorkers—and the country. After all, it is Manhattan's oldest public building in continuous use (it was built in 1766) and was George Washington's post-inauguration place of worship. And then the World Trade Center Towers, located just next door, came tumbling down, destroying everything in their path—except miraculously St. Paul's, which instantly became home base for firefighters, police and other rescue teams. In order to appreciate the full story and the enormity of 9/11, you should visit St. Paul's **"Unwavering Spirit" exhibit,** which takes over the entire church with artifacts from the nine-month period when St. Paul's was the makeshift site for volunteer relief efforts. Artifacts include poignant pictures of people who lost their lives that day, banners that were stitched with heartfelt thanks from people around the world to New York's bravest, audio and video tapes, and a cot where firefighters and policemen took respite. In the days immediately after 9/11, the church was lined with cots on which relief effort volunteers would place a stuffed animal for the firefighters and other rescue teams to take comfort.

National Museum of the American Indian

Smithsonian Institution, The George Gustav Heye Center, Alexander Hamilton U.S. Custom House. One Bowling Green (across from Battery Park), Tel. 212/514-3700, www.americanindian.si.edu.

Open: Daily 10am to 5pm. Open until 8pm on Thursday. Closed Christmas day.

Admission: Free.

Subway: 4, 5 to Bowling Green, 1 to South Ferry, N, R to Whitehall St. and M, J, Z to Broad Street.

The setting of this museum is one reason to visit—it's located in the historic U.S. Customs House building. Other reasons: live performances and films bring your kid's textbook pages to life. Bonus: Many of the guides are Native American.

The Tribute WTC Visitor Center

120 Liberty Street, 866/737-1184, www.tributewtc.org.

Open: Monday 10am to 6pm, Tuesday noon to 6pm, Wednesday through Saturday 10am to 6pm, Sunday noon to 5pm.

Admission: $10 recommended donation.

Subway: 2, 3, 4. 5, 6, A, E, R.

Your tip that you're near the site where the World Trade Center Towers once stood is the silence of the visitors who stroll and absorb the what-now-resembles a pit with construction equipment. The site is fenced in and you can walk around part of it. There has been a lot of controversy surrounding what will be built here, if anything. Some New Yorkers want to see another skyscraper; others view it as a burial ground that should be immortalized as a meditation park.

While the controversy continues to swirl at press time, redevelopment is underway for 7 World Trade Center with a 52-story building including a memorial and a Freedom Tower and new state-of-the-art transit center. The 1,776-foot Freedom Tower is expected to open in 2012 and will feature a 2.6 million square-foot office space, a rooftop restaurant and an observation deck. The three-level memorial is still in a design phase.

Especially poignant is **The Viewing Wall** here with the names of those who died, and 17 history panels that tell the story of the evolution of Manhattan from colonial times to today. You can also take a walking tour.

Winter Garden Atrium/World Financial Center

West Street (between Liberty and Vesey streets), Tel. 212/945-0505, www.worldfinancialcenter.com.

Subway: 1, 2, 3, E, N, R.

Located in Battery City Park on the Hudson River, The World Financial Center houses four office towers (including American Express and Merrill Lynch). The office towers are connected by a string of courtyards, including the spectacular **Winter Garden Atrium**. Here, there are great restaurants to eat in (Japanese, Chinese, steak, seafood, coffee, juice bar) and shops to explore (Banana Republic, Godiva, Ann Taylor). If it's a lovely day, grab a sandwich or made-your-way salad at Cosi (there are several Cosi shops around Manhattan; the fresh-from-the-oven bread is fantastic) and go outside to sit in one of the public gardens or along the Esplanade with river views.

Bonus: The Winter Garden Atrium is the stage for year-round performing arts festivals and performances. Check the website above for upcoming events.

Note: The World Financial Center and Winter Garden Atrium is a five-minute walk from Ground Zero. And, the Museum of Jewish Heritage (see next page) also makes its home here.

The Skyscraper Museum

39 Battery Place, Tel. 212/968-1961, www.skyscraper.org.

Open: Wednesday through Sunday noon to 6pm.

Admission: General $5, students and seniors $2.50.

Subway: 4 or 5 to Bowling Green, R or W to Whitehall St. 1 to Rector St.

Located on the ground floor of the Ritz-Carlton Hotel on the southern tip of Battery Park City, this museum is a tribute to New York's architectural heritage and the individuals behind it. It includes VIVA, a 3-

D Computer model of Manhattan and hosts family programs throughout the year. Bonus: Kids can go online and test their skyscraper IQ.

South Street Seaport

Visitor's Center is located at 209 Water Street (Fulton Street), Tel. 212/SEA-PORT, www.southstseaport.org.

Open: Tuesday through Sunday 10am to 6pm.; November through March open until 5pm Friday through Sunday. Closed Monday all year.

Admission: Free to the marketplace; to the museum—$8 adults, $6 seniors and students, $4 for kids five to twelve years old, free for kids under five years old.

Subway: 2, 3, 4, 5, A, C, J, M, Z.

A fantasy of upscale shops and eateries housed in a historic seaport and festive marketplace with ongoing live entertainment that's similar to Boston's Faneuil Hall and Quincy Market. There's also the **South Street Seaport Museum** here with buildings that house a tiny, children's museum, printing shop and boat-building shop. The best part: The historic ships that kids can climb aboard or you can take a cruise.

The Seaport also houses an ambitious and inexpensive food court on the top level of the complex with giant windows that peer out onto the harbor. The eateries are easy on the wallet and, we don't need to tell you that kids love food courts. Bonus: Visit at dusk to watch the moon rise behind the Brooklyn Bridge.

New York City Police Museum

100 Old Slip (four blocks south of South Street Seaport), Tel. 212/480-3100, www.nycpolicemuseum.org.

Open: Monday through Saturday 10am to 5pm. Closed Sunday.

Admission: (Suggested donation) Adults $5, seniors $3, kids (ages 6 to 18 years old) $2.

Subway: 4, 5 to Bowling Green, 1, 2 to Wall Street, N, R to Whitehall, South Ferry.

Way back when, the NYPD's 1st Precinct once called this museum home. Today, kids can learn about the history and the culture of New York's finest. There are permanent and rotating exhibits. Wall of Heroes is devoted to 9/11 and depicts the role that the New York Police Department played with on-camera interviews, photos and Ground Zero artifacts. In other exhibits, there's a Harley Davidson police motorcycle, shields, uniforms, a mugshot camera and a firearms training stimulator.

The Museum of Jewish Heritage—A Living Memorial to the Holocaust
   36 Battery (at Battery Park), Tel. 646/437-4200, www.mjhnyc.org.
   Open: Sunday through Tuesday and on Thursday 10am to 5:45pm, Wednesday 10am to 8pm, Friday 10am to 5pm (daylight savings time), Friday eve of Jewish holidays 10am to 3pm. Closed Saturday, Jewish holidays and Thanksgiving.
   Admission: $10 adults, $7 seniors, $5 students, kids 12 years old and under are free. Free admission every Wednesday from 4pm to 8pm.
   Subway: 4, 5, W, R, 1, J, M, Z.
   A museum that tells the story of Jews in the 21st century through a collection of personal objects, original films and other artifacts. The first and third floor house exhibits that are child friendly. However, the second floor exhibit, *The War Against The Jews* might be disturbing for young children and so the museum warns parents to visit the exhibit first before allowing their young kids to do the same. Nice touch: the Garden of Stones Memorial Garden in honor of Holocaust survivors and those who died (free and open to the public.)

   Children's workshops take place on Sundays and be sure to pick up the family guide (geared for children ages 7 to 11 years old), *"You Are A Museum Detective—The Case: Looking for Heritage in All the Right Places."*

   Bonus: The museum is also home to The Heritage Café, with a Kosher menu and great views of the Statue of Liberty.

Parent Tips

• Head to the top floor deck of Pier 17 which juts into the East River to recline in a deck chair and watch New York Harbor and the Brooklyn and Manhattan bridges.

• When you and the kids are pooped from too much pounding the pavement, jump on the Downtown Connection, a free bus service for visitors (as well as residents and workers). The route runs between South Street Seaport and northern Battery Park City. The best part: You can hop on and off the bus at designated stops.

National Sports Museum

26 Broadway, Tel. 212/837-7950, www.thesportsmuseum.org.

Subway: 2, 3, 4. 5, 6, A, E, R.

Said to be the first-ever, major comprehensive museum dedicated to sports was slated to open spring 2008 in lower Manhattan. The museum will be the permanent home of college football's biggest honor, the Hesiman Trophy. Hours and admission were unavailable at press time.

ELLIS ISLAND & THE STATUE OF LIBERTY

Liberty Island, Tel. 212/363-3200, www.nps.gov/stli.

Open: 9:30am to 5pm, although the hours are adjusted seasonally. Closed on Christmas. Note: as of press time, the crown and torch are not open.

Ferry: Circle Line ferry leaves Battery Park every hour on the hour daily. Round trip ferry cost: $12 kids and adults 13 years old and older, $10 seniors, $5 kids ages 4 to 12 years old, free kids 2 and under. You can purchase advance tickets by phone: 877/LADYTIX. You can also purchase advance tickets online at www.statuecruises.com. Ferries depart from New York City's Battery Park (Tel. 212/269-5755) and Jersey City's Liberty State Park (Tel. 201/435-9499). (See website for additional, up-to-date details.)

Subway to the ferry: 1.

Note: If you're short for time, the ferry from Manhattan stops first at the Statue of Liberty on its way to Ellis Island. You can disembark and catch a later ferry to Ellis Island. Or, you can take your photos from the boat and just continue onto Ellis Island.

The Statue of Liberty interior and museum was closed to visitors for a few years after September 11, 2001, although the grounds were open for strolling and viewing the statue. While visitors still cannot enter the interior of the Statue, in-cluding the crown and torch, they will be able to view the Statue's interior through a glass ceiling near the statue's base. You can go to the observation deck on top of the 16-foot pedestal to see the 360-degree view. Prior to 9/11, visitors were able to climb the

354 steps to the Statue's crown or 192 steps to the top of the pedestal.

The Statue of Liberty National Monument was a gift from the people of France to the people of the United States more than 100 years ago (she celebrated her 100th birthday in 1986) as a gesture of friendship between the two nations during the American Revolution. Through the years, the Statue has become a symbol of freedom and democracy and has welcomed many immigrants to this country.

A visit to the Statue of Liberty is an enriching and educational experience for kids. To enhance the visit, sign up for the **Junior Ranger Program**, a self-guided program for kids ages 7 to 12 (this is a recommended age range, but younger and older kids can also participate). Keep in mind for really young kids, getting to Lady Liberty really is half the fun—or the whole fun thanks to the salty, windy, sunny ferry ride over. The kids get a Junior Park Ranger Booklet that teaches them about the importance of the National Park Service and the Statue of Liberty through kid-friendly activities. The booklet takes about one hour to complete. They can download the booklet at www.nps.gov/stli or pick one up at the Information Center on Liberty Island. Activity sheets are also available for kids free or charge; you can pick them up from park rangers at the information center.

Lady Liberty Facts

- The length of Lady Liberty's index finger is 8 feet.
- The length of her hand is 16 feet and 5 inches.
- The length of her nose is 4 feet and 6 inches.
- The length from the ground to the tip of her torch is 305 feet and one inch.
- The thickness of her waist is 35 feet.
- There are 25 windows in her crown to symbolize gemstones found on the earth and the heaven's rays. The seven rays in the crown represent the seven seas and continents of the world.

There is more to the Statue of Liberty than the monument. There are also several museums on site. Located on the second floor of the pedestal is the **Statue of Liberty Exhibit**, which traces the history of the Statue through photos, videos and oral presentations. Kids will love the full-scale replicas of the Statue's foot and face that are on display here. There are also exhibits that explore the symbolism of the Statue. And a bronze plaque with the "New Colossus," a famous sonnet written by Emma Lazarus in 1883, is also housed here; Lazarus contributed to the completion of the Statue's pedestal.

The **Torch Exhibit** features the original 1886 torch and flame in the lobby. A complementary exhibit on the balcony's second floor details the history of the torch.

A visit to **Ellis Island** is interesting for school age kids and older. Twelve million immigrants passed through here between 1892 and 1954. In 1990, Ellis Island opened as a museum there.

A really cool, worthwhile thing to do: have your ancestors' names inscribed on the American Immigration Wall of Honor at Ellis Island. Note: Your relatives did not have to come through Ellis Island to this country; as long as they immigrated to the U.S. their names can be inscribed on the wall. You can do this either online (go to www.wallofhonor.com) or when you arrive. My mother had my grandparents' names (John and Christina Mackinnon MacDougall, Canada and Scotland) and (Santa and Anthony Freni Zimboni, Italy) inscribed on the Wall. Cost: $150 each name. For more information call Donor Service at Tel. 212/561-4588.

There is a cafeteria that sells sandwiches and snacks. But, if you plan ahead, you'll grab a couple of pastrami or corned beef deli sandwiches in Manhattan before jumping on the ferry; there are plenty of perfect-picnic-perches on Liberty Island and Ellis Island.

THE BOWERY

Once the armpit of Manhattan, home to the homeless when they were "bums" as well as squeegee window washers when they were legal (pre-Guilliani era), the Bowery has evolved somewhat to a kinder, gentler part of town—especially recently when the New Museum opened here.

The New Museum

235 Bowery (at Prince Street), 212/219-1222, www.newmuseum.org.

Open: Wednesday noon to 6pm, Thursday and Friday noon to 10pm, Saturday and Sunday noon to 6pm.

Admission: $12 adult, $8 seniors, $6, free for kids 18 years old and younger. Budget Tip: Thursday evenings between 7pm and 10pm is pay what you wish.

Subway: 6 to Spring Street or N/R to Prince Street.

A new cutting-edge, contemporary art museum that is turning heads in this once-aesthetically void neighborhood. Free docent tours are given and on the first Saturday of each month, there's a creative arts program where kids (six to 15 years old) take thematic tours and participate in creative activities; there is a 10am and an 11am session. Advance registration is required. For more information call 212/219-1222, ext. 235. Bonus: The glass-enclosed rooftop lounge where you can buy beverages.

4. BETWEEN TRIBECA & 14th STREET

In a word: Cool. This funky, trendy part of town is always tops on the list of teens. Think: body piercing, blue and green hair, revealing clothing and a got-to-be-me vibe. This is the City's hipster spot. I've lived in both Soho and Greenwich Village and loved every minute.

When I lived in Soho right out of college, it was sleepy and very neighborhoody with wonderful galleries and unique shops that attracted visitors on spring, summer and fall weekends. Soho's had a major wake-up call (critics call it a rude awakening) but I still love it down here. It's certainly not as sleepy, but it's still appealing. Peanut Butter and Company (*see photo on page 41*) is on Soho's Sullivan Street, one of the city's most popular kid-friendly eateries.

See map on pages 28-29 for locations in this chapter.

Parent Tips

• The Scholastic Store in Soho is a fun-loving kids-only bookstore that stocks not only educational toys and books, but that also has an activity loft where workshops, musical performances and storytelling are held. Most of the events are geared to the preschool set. Located at 557 Broadway (near Prince Street), Tel. 212/343-6166.

• Bloomingdale's has made its home on the East Side for years, and now it's got a downtown sidekick; a sister store in Soho. The new Bloomies is much smaller than its uptown sibling and has a downtown, Soho edge to it. Located at 504 Broadway (between Spring and Broome Streets); Tel. 212/729-5900, www.bloomingdales.com.

• Buy the ultimate souvenir while visiting NoHo at Bond No. 9 New York. The shop sells custom fragrances named after New York City neighborhoods, from Park Avenue to the Lower East Side to Chelsea—or a combo of several of your favorite neighborhoods. Located at 9 Bond Street, Tel. 212/228-1732. Also located on the Upper East Side and in the Village.

Lower East Side
Tenement Museum
108 Orchard Street (at Broome Street), Tel. 212/431-0233, www.tenement.org.

Open: The main Gallery is open daily 11am to 5:30pm; afternoon tours run often Tuesday through Fridays, 1:20pm to 5pm and Saturday and Sunday beginning at 11:15am until 4:45pm.

Admission: Free admission to Gallery. Tours: $17 adults, $13 students and seniors.

Subway: B, D, F, J, M, Z.

Manhattan's Lower East Side once served as a "Gateway to America," and this museum depicts those early days. Recreated tenement apartments that tell the tales of immigrants are set up to depict the cramped, impoverished living quarters that these immigrants experienced. To fully absorb the story, it's best to take one of the tours. The best: *The Confino Family Apartment,* based on the Sephardic-Jewish Confino family from Kastoria (once part of the Ottoman Empire, now in Greece.) An interpreter in full costume plays the part of teenager Victoria Confino in 1916. She welcomes museum visitors as though you had just arrived from your homeland and teaches you how to adapt to America. Lively and educational for all ages.

Note: The Confino program costs $17 adults, $13 students and seniors. The Confino program takes place on afternoon weekends; advance reservations are not required, but you can do so. Visit the website or call for exact times.

Forbes Magazine Galleries

60 Fifth Avenue (at 12th Street), Tel. 212/206-5548, www.forbesgalleries.com.

Open: Tuesday, Wednesday, Friday and Saturday 10am to 4pm. Closed Sunday, Monday and Thursday and major holidays.

Admission: Free (No strollers).

Subway: F, L, N, Q, R.

There are two operative words for families thinking of visiting this museum: toys and free (no, not free toys!). You don't have to pay to enter this small gem of a museum that's a showcase for Forbes' collection of toy boats and soldiers, as well as his quirky collection of Monopoly games, medals and trophies, and Presidential papers (Forbes was a compulsive collector).

Children's Museum of the Arts

182 Lafayette Street (between Broome and Grand streets), Tel. 212/274-0986, www.cmany.org.

Open: Wednesday, Friday, Saturday and Sunday, noon to 5pm, Thursday 12 to 6pm

Admission: $9; pay-what-you-wish on Thursday 4pm to 6pm.

Subway: 6, N, R.

A sweet museum that's much smaller than the Upper West Side Children's Museum, this downtown spot has many programs and events for kids throughout the year (check the website or call for updates). Permanent attractions include a Performing Arts Gallery (kids perform on camera and are shown on a screen), a Creative Play Area (for kids 5 years and under,) and a Ball Pond (for kids of all ages) that's a cushioned space with large physio balls. The Upper West Side children's museum is more popular, but this low-key downtown museum that is celebrating its 20th anniversary, doesn't tend to get super crowded.

5. CHELSEA

There's not a whole lot of stuff going on for kids in this lively neighborhood except for Chelsea Piers, which kids and adults adore (*photo below*). But that's about to change with the much-anticipated Fall 2008 opening of the High Line, a hip, elevated public promenade that will span 1.5 miles and 22 blocks, much of which will travel through or above Chelsea. Starting at Gansevoort Street in the Meatpacking District and traveling up the West Side of Manhattan to 34th Street, the High Line will woo kids with plenty of running around space with secret gardens, green parks, and awesome views of the Manhattan skyline and the Hudson River. The sunsets from this perch should be life-changing. New Yorkers fought hard to preserve this stretch of neglected railway.

Chelsea has also become an interesting place for tweens and teens kids to window shop and poke around in some of the galleries. If you get hungry or it's raining, the Chelsea Market is a fun place to spend some time (*see photo on page 44*).

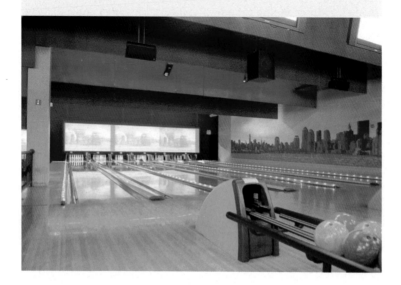

Chelsea Piers

West 23rd Street (at the Hudson River), Tel. 212/336-6666, www.chelseapiers.com.

Open: The operating schedule varies depending on the activity. Call or visit the website for specific information.

Admission: The cost depends on the activity. Call or visit the website for specific information.

Subway: C, E.

Sporty New York families practically live at this sprawling 30-acre sports and recreation complex with baseball hitting cages, ice-skating rinks (see entry under skating), basketball courts, a driving range (see entry under golf), indoor soccer fields, bowling, a rock-climbing wall and lots more.

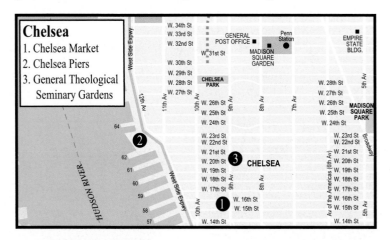

Chelsea

1. Chelsea Market
2. Chelsea Piers
3. General Theological Seminary Gardens

Parent Tip

A nice contrast to the Chelsea Pier Complex is the off-the-beaten-path gardens at the General Theological Seminary of the Episcopal Church on Ninth Avenue (between 20th and 21st streets). The Seminary property, which dates back to 1827 was donated by Clement Clark Moore, a professor at the Seminary and, of course, the alleged author of the famous poem which begins, "'Twas the night before Christmas." The 32,000-square-foot garden that's home to 60 trees, 35 flowerbeds and a handful of benches is a perfect respite from the busy streets of Manhattan. The gardens are open Monday through Friday between noon and 3pm and Saturday between 11am and 3pm, closed on Sunday. Bonus: **Billy's Bakery**, home to amazing cupcakes and other sweet gooey goodies, is a cupcake-throw away at 184 9th Avenue and West 21st (Tel. 212/647-9956).

6. TIMES SQUARE & THEATER DISTRICT

Times Square and the surrounding Theater District has morphed into a lively, safe family mecca, thanks to a total facelift and renovation project spearheaded by former Mayor Rudolph Guliani. There are tons of family activities in Times Square, as well as family-friendly restaurants and hotels. In fact, *USA Today* named Times Square one of the top 10 places in the United States to visit. That is just incredible considering ten years ago Times Square was a place recommended to stay *far away from* when visiting the City.

See map on page 51 for locations in this chapter.

ESPN Zone
1472 Broadway, Tel. 212/921-ESPN, www.espnzone.com.
Open: Sunday 11am to 11pm, Monday through Friday 11:30am to midnight, Saturday 11am to midnight.
Subway: 1, 2, 3, 7, A, C, E, N, R (to Times Square Station).
This is my all-sports-all-the-time son's favorite place to visit in Manhattan and if your son or daughter love sports, they'll love it here, too. Think: baseball, soccer, basketball, hockey, interactive games (Mad Wave Motion Theater and RPM 2 Night) and a fun restaurant, too. It's a super stimulating environment (translation: it can get nuts with lots of teens and kids), especially during the summer and school breaks. (No one under the age of 18 is allowed in the gaming room without an adult.) The restaurant doesn't take reservations and there's often a line at peak hours so think about eating when it first opens and then hitting the games (see dining section for more info). There are 100 flat screen and HDTV's for viewing sports events including two 14-foot HDTV screens in the screening room and flat screen TV's in the grill. Live radio and TV shows are often taped from here and it's not unusual to see athletes and sports celebs.

Toys 'R Us Times Square
1514 Broadway (44th and 45th), 800/869-7787, www4.toysrus.com/timessquare.
Open: Monday through Thursday 10am to 10pm, Friday and Saturday 10am to 11pm, Sunday 11am to 9pm.
Subway: 1, 2, 3, 7, A, C, E, N, R (to Times Square Station).
This three-story store is big. How big? Big enough for a larger-than-life, full-size, indoor Ferris wheel. At peak times, they line up down the block for a spin on the wheel (hard to believe but true). This Toys 'R Us is atypical of the chain's other stores—if you use your imagination, think of it as a toy store/museum dedicated to Manhattan. There's a fabulous scale model of New York City landmarks in the Lego section, a life-size Barbie dollhouse and a five-ton, 20-foot-high robotic T-Rex. Tickets for the Ferris wheel are $2.50, free for kids less than 2 years old. Note: Kids under 40 inches must be accompanied on the ride by an adult. Kids also love the new R Zone, a 5,000-square-foot zone that features the latest and greatest electronic games with huge plasma screens.

Madame Tussaud's New York
234 West 42nd Street, 800/246-8872, www.madame-tussauds.com.
Open: Sunday through Thursday 10am to 8pm, Friday 10am to

10pm (open 365 days a year). Call to confirm because the museum sometimes closes early for special events and there are also extended summer hours.

Admission: Adults (13 to 59 years old) $29, kids (4 to 12 years old) $23, seniors (60 years and older) $26, kids under four years old are free.

Subway: 1,2,3,7,A,C,E,N, R (to Times Square Station).

Woody Allen, Joe DiMaggio, Whoopi Goldberg and Derek Jeter are all here, as well as tons of other New York-loving celebs including two of the newest, rapper Biggie Smalls (B.I.G.) and Met's heartthrob David Wright. There's also the popular interactive wax figure: a blushing Jennifer Lopez (J Lo). Whisper something to her and watch her blush (oh my God!) And, of course, there's an American Idol attraction. The "museum" features more than 200 life-size wax figures of celebrities in theme environments, including sports, theater and entertainment. This is a great photo-op spot. Caveat: Young kids, seven and under, might be spooked by the wax effigies.

The prices are steep, but you can spend a good chunk of time here and will get your money's worth.

MTV Studios

1515 Broadway between 44th and 45th Streets, Tel. 212/258-8000.
Subway: 1, 2, 3, 7, A, C, E, N, R (to Times Square Station).

Teens gather outside this popular studio on weekdays to sneak a peek of *Total Request Live* heartthrob host Carson Daly. Note: The studio is not on street level so it's hard to see much of anything. But that won't stop your teen from trying (*see photo on next page*).

E-Walk (Entertainment Walk)

247 West 42nd Street, 212/50L-OEWS.
Subway: A,C,E, N,Q,R,W,4

Teens especially love this 200,000-square-foot entertainment complex that is connected by five interconnected bridges. You'll find 13 movie theaters, several restaurants including Chevy's Fresh Mex and B.B. Kings restaurant and blues venue and the huge Broadway City Arcade. The Westin Hotel is also attached.

7. MIDTOWN

Midtown Manhattan is a sprawling business district and home to many hotels, shops and restaurants. Midtown is all about hustle bustle. If you're out for a family stroll between noon and 2pm when the corporate world crawls out of its cubicles for air and lunch— expect impatient workers who can't believe you're actually walking *so* slowly, impeding their quick, grab-a-bite-to-eat-lunch. For seven years I worked as a travel editor at a magazine that's located at 54th Street and Fifth Avenue. My co-workers would swap horror stories about how unbearable and intolerable the crammed sidewalks are, especially during the holidays when tourists would clog the area to admire the store windows dressed for the holidays and the fabulous tree at **Rockefeller Center**, a few blocks away. I must admit, though, I never knew what all the fuss was and actually loved the spirit of the visitors who were out and about enjoying the City that New Yorkers all too often take for granted.

Bryant Park
40 to 42nd Street, Fifth to Sixth Avenues, Tel. 212/768-4242,
www.bryantpark.org.
Subway: F,V,B,D (to 42nd Street), 7 (to Fifth Avenue), 1,2, 3, A, C,
E, N, R (to Times Square).
Think a slice of Paris in New York. The New York Public Library's
backyard, Bryant Park used to be a major drug den in the 1970's (during
those years I once had to hit the pavement while walking by because of a
shooting). But, it's been cleaned up and has become one of the cities most
popular parks for outdoor concerts, like the annual **Broadway Under the
Stars** summer kickoff concert. The Bryant Park lawn is as big as a football
field (300 feet long and 215 feet wide). Because of its midtown location,
expect lots of office workers eating take-out salads and sandwiches at
lunchtime on pretty spring, summer and fall days. (There are also four
kiosks throughout the park with fabulous offerings created by some of the
city's best chefs). And, the Park recently added an ice skating rink in winter.
     The Park's kinship to France is evident in the London plane trees that
are planted along the twin promenades (these are the same species of trees
at the Jardin des Tuileries in Paris). Bonus: Every Monday night during the
summer months, outdoor movies are shown for free. Also during the
summer, *Good Morning America* hosts free Friday morning concerts in
Bryant Park. And, during Fashion Week each spring you'll spy tents set up
for the lineup of non-stop fashion shows.
     The real draw for young kids here is **Le Carrousel**, a French-inspired
carousel that twirls to French cabaret music; the carousel is located mid-Park
on the 40th street side. The cost: $1.75 per ride. You'll also find chess and
backgammon tables, and free wireless access (if you have a laptop or handheld
device). In keeping with the French theme, the game of Petangue, a French
game of boules is played on a gravel path (free petangue lessons are given
Monday through Friday 11:30am to 2pm). Unique to Bryant Park is an
outdoor reading room, open daily from 11am to 5pm, weather permitting.
     Combine a trip to Bryant Park with a visit to the main branch of the
New York Public Library (there are actually 85 libraries as part of the New
York Public Library system in the Bronx, Manhattan and Staten Island).
This formidable building houses a dizzying collection of books, and it also
is the scene for free children's workshops and storytelling hours. Before you
visit Manhattan, call Tel. 212/621-0636 or visit www.nypl.org/events to
request a brochure for library events that will take place during your visit.
     Bonus: The bathrooms at Bryant Park were awarded the "best in
America" by City Search. They are incredibly clean and pretty. Yes, pretty.

**Theater District/
Times Square/Midtown**

1. Build-A-Bear Workshop
2. Bryant Park
3. Empire State Building
4. ESPN Zone
5. FAO Schwarz
6. Fire Department New York
   Fire Zone
7. Grand Central Terminal
8. Intrepid Sea-Air Space Museum
9. Madame Tussaud's New York
10. Museum of Modern Art (MoMA)
11. Museum of Television and Radio
12. MTV Studios
13. NBC Experience Studio Tours
14. New York Public Library
15. Rockefeller Center
16. SONY Wonder Technology Lab
17. Toys 'R Us
18. United Nations

Empire State Building

350 Fifth Avenue, Tel. 212/736-3100, www.esbnyc.com.

Open: Daily, 365 days a year, from 8am to 2am (last elevator leaves at 11:15pm).

Admission: $17.61 adults 18 years old to 61 years old, $15.76 seniors 62 years old and older, $15.76 kids 12 years old to 17 years old, $12.07 kids 6 years old to 11, free for kids ages five and younger. Audio tour: $7 per person.

Subway: 1, 2, 3 (to Seventh Avenue), A, C, E (to 34th Street/Penn Station), B, D, F, N, Q, R (to 34th Street/Avenue of the Americas.

In a word: View. This Art Deco building on 34th Street gives visitors an eagle's eye view of Manhattan—and beyond (on a clear day, you can spy Massachusetts!). When the World Trade Center buildings stood tall, you could take in the views from the observation deck there. Now, the Empire State Building is the only gig in town.

High-powered binoculars are available for a minimal cost. You'll reach the **86th floor observatory**, which is 1,050 feet up by a high-speed elevator. The **102nd floor has viewing** from 1,250 feet above Manhattan, too, which was closed to public following 9/11 for several years but which has reopened. It costs $15 extra and features a glass-enclosed area and an open-air promenade. Tip: When you arrive in the city, check the local weather and plan your trip to the top of the Empire State Building accordingly—

sunny, cloudless days rule.

Also make time for the **Skyride** attraction, a large flight stimulator that takes visitors on a sweeping aerial tour of Manhattan with Kevin Bacon as the spaceship's captain.

We love the idea that you never know what colors the Empire State Building's three-tiered lighting tower will display. For instance, when the Yankees won the World Series it was lighted up in blue and white. You can even request a special color lighting for an occasion dear to your heart, keeping in mind that tons of requests are received each year. Note: Birthdays and anniversaries are not honored.

If you see the tower lights turned off during the spring or fall it could be to deter birds from flying into the building. Spring and fall are prime bird migration seasons. If a large number of birds are reported flying near the building, observatory personnel at the outdoor deck on the 86th floor report the sighting to the engineers who turn the lights off (birds are attracted to lights).

Bonus: The Empire State Building's audio tour, narrated by a fictitious New Yorker who *tawks* about the City's landmarks, neighborhoods and attractions. The tour is available in eight languages.

Never-before-seen-areas of the *Intrepid* including berthing quarters will be open to the public, and new interactive exhibits will also be featured.

Budget Tip: Save some bucks and buy the ESP Observatory & New York Skyride Combo Package. To buy it online, go to www.esbnyc.com.

Fire Department New York Fire Zone

34 West 51st Street (between 5th and 6th avenues), Tel. 212/698-4520, www.fdnyfirezone.com. (Located adjacent to Radio City Music Hall at Rockefeller Center).

Open: Monday through Saturday 9am to 7pm, Sundays and holidays 11am to 5pm. Note: At times the museum is taken over by school groups; call ahead to make sure it is open to the public when you'd like to visit.

Admission: General admission is free. Fire simulation presentation costs $6 adults and kids, $2 seniors 60 years old and older.

Subway: B, D, E, F, V.

This is an educational yet fun fire safety learning center for kids of all ages. Through a guided multi-media tour led by a firefighter, kids—and adults—learn how to crawl through a smoke-filled, dark room, feel for a hot door, identify hazards in their own home and, ultimately plan escape routes in their home.

Intrepid Sea, Air, Space Museum

Pier 86 (46th and West Side Highway), Tel. 212/245-0072, www.intrepidmuseum.com.

Subway: A, C, E. 42nd Street/Port Authority.

Note: The Intrepid is closed until Veteran's Day 2008.

Don't tell them it's a museum, or you're sunk. This 900-foot-long aircraft carrier is actually so not a museum. Tell them about the landing deck with the small planes, helicopters and jets—some of which kids can climb into. Calling all boys: below deck there's an awesome F-18 fighter jet simulator. True, there are "museumy" displays of uniforms, weapons and navy memorabilia. Note: the submarine USS Growler (guided tours only; must be at least six years old; at press time, however, the USS Growler was off-site). There are also 25 aircraft (early wooden to supersonic jetfighters, including the Concorde.) Your kids will have lots of questions to ask and thankfully World War II Veterans are often on hand to oblige.

NBC Experience Store/Studio Tours

30 Rockefeller Plaza (49th Street between 5th and 6th avenues across from Studio A, the Today Show home), Tel. 212/664-3700, www. NBC.com.

Open: Monday through Thursday: 8:30am to 4:30pm, Friday and Saturday, 9:30am to 5:30pm and Sunday 9:30am to 4:30pm, closed Thanksgiving and Christmas. Note: Kids under six years old not admitted.

Admission: $18.50 adults, $15.50 seniors and kids age 6 to 16 years old. Note: Kids under the age of six years are not admitted.

Subway: 47th-50th streets/Rockefeller Center B, D, F, S; 49th Street N,R,W; 50th Street 1.

Take a behind-the-scenes guided tour of the studios where *Saturday Night Live, Late Night with Conan O'Brien and Dateline NBC* are produced. Great tour for star struck visitors—you never know which anchor or celeb you'll bump into. Plus, there's neat interactive stuff: be a meteorol-ogist and do the weather with Al Roker, test your sports trivia knowledge with sports anchor Bob Costas, or, "sit" next to Jay Leno at the *Tonight Show*. **Bonus:** Each interactive experience is free; you can opt to purchase a videotape.

The **NBC store** on the street level floor sells NBC merchandise, including T-shirts, mugs, etc. from shows like *30 Rock* and *Deal or No Deal*. The second level houses a sweets shop—strategically situated next to where you'll line up for the tour.

Want to be part of the *Today Show*? See my Parent Tip on the next page!

Parent Tip

Want to wave a big hello to grandma back home in Omaha? Get up real early and head for the plaza outside of *The Today Show*'s glass-enclosed studio. The stars often go out to meet and greet during the live show (it starts at 7am). Bonus: Come on a Friday in the summer and catch one of the **concerts**. It's a great way to start a fabulous New York City day. For the best view, go to the southwest corner of 49th Street and Rockefeller Center). For an up-to-date schedule of *Today* concerts, go to www.msnbc.msn.com.

SONY Wonder Technology Lab
550 Madison Avenue (56th Street), Tel. 212/833-8100, www.sonywondertechlab.com.
Open: Tuesday through Saturday, 10am to 5pm, closed Sunday and Monday.
Admission: Free.
Subway: 4, 5, 6, N, E, R.
Note: SONY Wonder Technology Lab is closed for a major upgrading until August, 2008. However, the 2nd floor remains open for the duration where you'll find music, films and video game exhibits.

Grand Central Terminal
42nd Street and Park Avenue (between Lexington and Vanderbilt Avenues), Tel. 212/340-2210, www.grandcentralterminal.com.
Subway: S (shuttle), 4, 5, 6 ,7.
Built between 1903 and 1913 by a Minnesota architectural firm, this stunning train terminal is one of the City's most famous landmarks and a hotbed of activity with commuters, restaurants, shops and live entertainment. Grand Central is also tops on most tourists' must-see list.

The late Jacqueline Kennedy Onassis was Grand Central's staunchest supporter and she worked hard to save the structure from demolition that also paved the way for the legality of New York's landmark preservation law. Thanks to her help, Grand Central was restored during the 1990's. Today, it's worth a peek to see the

12-story ceiling that displays stars and the gilded constellations of the zodiac, as well as to grab a bite in the illustrious Oyster Bar where you can slurp down over 30 varieties of oysters. Steak-and-potatoes-kind-of-folks will slam-dunk at Michael Jordan's The Steakhouse; the views of the Terminal will also score points. There is a collection of stores, too.

Tip: You can tour Grand Central (see tours listings), or just pop in for a stroll through. There's also a satellite branch of the New York Transit Museum (located in Brooklyn) at Grand Central. If you want to witness a quintessential New York scene, visit about 8am or 5pm on a weekday and you'll see a buzz of commuter activity.

United Nations

First Avenue to the East River, and between 42nd 48th streets (Visitor's Center located at First Avenue and 46th Street), Tel. 212/963-TOUR, www.un.org/tours.

Open: Tours: Monday through Friday 9:30am to 4:45pm, Saturday and Sunday 10am to 4:30pm (Closed weekends in January and February and major holidays).

Admission: $13.50 adults, $9 seniors, $9 students, $7 kids 5 years old to 14 years old, kids under 5 not admitted.

Subway: 4, 5, 6, 7 to Grand Central Station.

If your kids are old enough (elementary school age through teen), they'll appreciate the guided, 45-minute long tour led by young men and women representing 37 countries. The tour visits the General Assembly Hall, the chambers of the Security Council, the Social Council, and international art exhibits including tapestries and mosaics (look for the Marc Chagall stained-glass window and Norman Rockwell mosaic). You might observe a meeting in progress—an average of 5,000 meetings are held annually; of course, some are closed to the public.

The U.N. actually spans 18 acres: Take a walk along the **promenade**, which fronts the East River; if it's late spring or summer check out the 1,400 rosebushes and sculptures donated by member nations. Which nations? Their flags fly in alphabetical order in the plaza. Your best bet for seeing delegates is to eat in the **Delegates' Dining Room**—if you don't see any delegates, at least you'll enjoy the view of the East River (you'll need to dress for the occasion—no shorts or sneakers and jackets are required for men.) The best time of year to experience the workings of the U.N. is when the **General Assembly** is in session, beginning the third Tuesday in September until late December. Another exciting time to visit the U.N. is when there are protests staged outside.

If you think your school-age child is too young to grasp the significance of a U.N. tour, think again. One guide poignantly recalls a tour she led on which there were two kids, eight and nine years old with their parents and a group of others. At one of the exhibits, she asked the group if they knew what an anti-personnel landmine was and how much did they think one would cost. None of the adults volunteered an answer and finally one of the kids said, "It costs you your life."

If you're pressed for time or have kids younger than five years old (they aren't allowed to take the tour), you can still visit the United Nations. At the **Visitor's Lobby** there is a free exhibit with rotating themes on display. The Visitor's Lobby is open Monday through Sunday, 9am to 5pm, March through December; during January and February it is open only Monday through Friday. To see which exhibits are being displayed while you plan to visit, go to www.un.org/events/UNART.

> ## Parent Tip
>
> Before you set out to visit the U.N., tell the kids you'll all be going out of the country for awhile. **The United Nations is not in the United States**; it sits in an international zone whose land belongs to all countries that have joined the Organization. The U.N. has its own security and fire department, and even its own postage stamps. Its six official languages are Arabic, Chinese, English, French, Russian and Spanish. Bonus: A terrific **gift shop** with items from many countries that make nice holiday gifts or souvenirs.

Rockefeller Center

47th to 52nd Streets (between Fifth and Sixth Avenues), Tel. 212/632-3975, www.rockefellercenter.com.

Subway: B, D, E, F, V.

Rockefeller Center is the core of the Big Apple. Built by the Rockefeller family in the 1930's, there are many ways to enjoy this tourist-must-see spot. Start at the **Channel Gardens**, which change with the seasons—during the holidays the Channel Gardens become home to a fantasy of angels. This is a perfect photo-op spot, as well as a place to sit, relax and watch the throng of tourists and office workers out for a stroll. Walk west through the gardens and you'll come to **Rockefeller Plaza**, anchored by the mammoth gilded statue of the Greek god Prometheus. Beneath the statue is one of the city's prettiest—and priciest—skating rinks. During Christmas the celebrated Christmas tree shadows Prometheus.

The NBC TV network is housed in the skyscraper just beyond the tree; limos pull up to drop off or pick up celeb types throughout the day. You can tour the studios; *The Today Show* tapes live at the studio to the south of the tree (see NBC Studio Tour entry). If it's a nice day, my son and I grab something delicious (soups, salads, sandwiches, pastries) to-go at **Dean & DeLuca** (a gourmet take-out shop) just across the street from *The Today Show* studio and eat our meal at one of the benches in Rockefeller Center. If the weather stinks, you can eat upstairs at Dean & DeLuca's— try to snag a window table that faces *The Today Show* studio for a celeb-spotting (of course, you may also find yourselves rubbing elbows with one at the next table). Or, opt to eat inside 30 Rockefeller Center at a handful of restaurants in the underground concourse, including such family-friendly eateries as **Two Boots** (Mexican). Tip: Hit the **Teuscher Chocolate shop** located next to the Channel Gardens for to-die-for Swiss truffles, about $1 a pop.

Top of the Rock

30 Rockefeller Plaza, 212/698-2000, www.rockefellercenter.com

Open: 365 days a year 8am to midnight

Admission: Adults $17.50, Children six to twelve years old $11.25, and Seniors $16

Subway: B, D, E, F, V

The newest observation deck to debut in New York offers visitors a 360-degree peek at the city from atop the 70-story GE Building. The deck, which was first opened in 1933, has been redeveloped to become a 55,000 square foot, multi-level complex with multi-media exhibits, an indoor viewing area and safety glass panels that allow for unobstructed open-air views of the city's most prominent landmarks.

The Paley Center for Media

25 West 52nd Street (5th and 6th Avenues), Tel. 212/621-6600, www.mtr.org.

Open: Tuesday through Sunday noon to 6pm, Thursday open until 8pm. Closed Monday.

Admission: Adults $10, $8 students and seniors, $5 kids 14 years old and under.

Subway: E, V.

This museum is candy for couch potato kids. What kid wouldn't want to spend a couple of hours watching TV? Arrive early and reserve a tape to search and select from a huge database you'd like to view or listen to in an individual console. The Beatles on *The Ed Sullivan Show,* the last episode of *Seinfeld,* footage of man landing on the moon, it's all here—in fact, there are over 140,000 television and radio programs and advertisements that date to the 1920s. There are also ongoing workshops for kids on Saturdays.

Museum of Modern Art

11 West 53rd Street (between 5th and 6th Avenues), Tel. 212/708-9400, www.moma.org.

Open: Saturday, Sunday, Monday Wednesday, Thursday 10:30am to 5:30pm, Friday 10:30am to 8pm, closed Tuesdays and Thanksgiving and Christmas.

Admission: $20 adults, $16 seniors, $12 students and kids 16 years old and under are free with an adult. Friday between 4pm and 8pm is free.

Subway: E, F.

Modern art lovers rejoice—MOMA is back and bigger and better than ever. In fact, it doubled in size. The lower level is home to two state-of-the-art theaters. The second floor displays contemporary art exhibits, including galleries for prints and illustrated books, a media gallery and a bookstore reading room. The museum's third floor houses gallery space for architecture and design, photos, drawings and temporary exhibits. Paintings and sculpture accent the fourth and fifth floor galleries. And the sixth floor showcases temporary exhibits in its expansive skylighted spaces. There are also a very popular fine dining restaurant and two cafes in the museum.

Ford Family Programs include guided tours, artists' talks and workshops; call 212/708-9805 for more information.

Friday nights at the movies—just for teens—is a popular event (think *Psycho* and other classic films) and there's a teen studio, too. No need to sign up, just drop in; runs from 4pm to 8pm and includes pizza and soda—all for free for high school students.

Caveat: This is one of the most expensive museums in the City to visit and unaffordable for many families.

Parent Tips

• Got a teenage girl who balks at museums with pouty lips that have been glossed over every half-hour? Make her day with a stop at the **Sephora** store in Times Square, a giant makeup store with cosmetics from brand companies. I love browsing here. For more info, visit www.sephora.com.

• Is there an elementary age girl, four years old or older in tow? The three-story **American Girl Place** on Fifth Avenue (at 49th street, across from Rockefeller Center) is a larger-than-life dollhouse. The **American Girl Café** here, done up in a black-and-white décor, serves meals all day for kids—and their dolls (and parents who indulge the stage their child is going through). Bonus: A treat seat for your daughter's doll. The cost for brunch is $19 per person (no, you don't have to pay for the doll) and includes cinnamon buns, French toast, pancakes, eggs benedict and sweet surprises (signature chocolate mousse flowerpot). Or, opt for lunch at $23 per person which includes fruit and cheese, a second course choice of items such as mini hamburger and cheeseburgers and a sweet surprises ending. Dinner at $25 per person is also offered, as is afternoon tea for $20 per person with scones and tea sandwiches made of egg salad, cream chees and cucumber, and that signature mousse flowerpot. Reserve in advance.

• If your daughter is a real doll, consider taking her to *The Circle of Friends: An American Girl Musical* here, a musical that brings the historical dolls to life in a 134-seat theater right in the store. The 75-minute show costs $34 a ticket. Get this: Visit the American Girl Store website (listed below) and plan an itinerary for your daughter and her doll. Hmm, does the doll want a new hairdo? If so, be prepared to shell out between $10 and $20. Call 877/AG-PLACE or visit www.americangirl.com. Open: Monday through Thursday 10am to 7pm, Friday 10am to 9pm, Saturday 9am to 9pm and Sunday 9am to 7pm.

The Plaza Hotel

The Plaza, one of the City's most celebrated hotels has gotten a socialite's facelift and recently debuted as a hotel and condo property. Room rates are exorbitant—beginning at $1,000 a night—and out of reach for most families. However, take time to visit the Plaza, especially if your kids are familiar with the classic piece of children's literature, *Eloise*. Also have a drink at the Oak Room and enjoy afternoon tea at Palm Court.

Build-A-Bear Workshop
565 Fifth Avenue (at 46th street), Tel. 212/871-7080, www.buildabear.com.
Subway: B, D, F, V

A big bear hug to this interactive shopping destination where kids make their own stuffed animal friends, personalizing them with fashion items and accessories. There's also a café with the usual suspects on the menu like hot dogs. Kids love this place.

FAO Schwarz
767 Fifth Avenue (at 58th Street), Tel. 212/644-9400, www.fao.com.

Open: Monday through Saturday 10am to 7pm, Sunday 11am to 6pm.

Subway: N, R.

Yes, this is a toy store, but it's one of the City's most popular tourist destinations, too. In fact, most people visit this store just to check it out, rather than buy anything—the toys are very pricey here. You'll be greeted outside by a real-life toy soldier and, if you're visiting during the holidays, expect to wait in line outside. I love the life-scale-size stuffed animals—kids love to give them a hug. Boys get revved up at the Hotel Wheels Factory where they can make their own cars, girls especially appreciate the Barbie Styled by Me where they can design their own Barbie dolls and wizards are keen on the Harry Potter shop. Kids also love the **candy department** on the first floor. Bonus: Belly up to the café.

8. UPPER EAST SIDE

The City's chicest neighborhood is where you'll find pricey boutiques, restaurants and hotels, as well as a collection of fabulous museums. The real beauty of the **Upper East Side** is that it borders Central Park—a playground for the rich and famous who live nearby. I lived on East 83rd Street and there wasn't a day—no matter the cold temps or rainy skies—that I wouldn't run around the Reservoir or walk through the Park on my way to work on the West Side. Central Park is good for the soul—in a town that moves quicker than a heartbeat.

The Metropolitan Museum of Art
Fifth Avenue (82nd Street), Tel. 212/535-7710, www.metmuseum.org.
Open: Friday 9:30am to 9:00pm, Saturday 9:30am to 9:00pm, Sunday, Tuesday, Wednesday, Thursday 9:30am to 5:30pm, Monday closed except Columbus Day, Christmas week, Martin Luther King Jr. Day, President's Day and Memorial Day.
Admission: Suggested donation of $20 adults, $15 students and senior citizens (this includes admission to The Cloisters on the same day.) Free to children under twelve with an adult, as well as to members. Strollers are permitted during regular Museum hours, although many of the exhibitions can't accommodate strollers. Back carriers are available to borrow at coat check areas at the 81st and 82nd Street entrances.
Subway: 4, 5, 6.
Operative words for getting your kids jazzed about spending time in this art museum: mummies, tombs, The **Temple of Dendur** in the Egyptian wing (kids can go into parts of the Temple and throw coins into the reflecting pools that surround it), giant, colorful sculptures on the roof garden and medieval armor. If that doesn't do it, mention the **Ancient Playground** next door with slides, rope and tires swings, sandbox and a water sprinkler. Need more bribery, um, persuasion tips? Tell them they give you two hours at the Met and you give them a trip to the City's most outrageous candy store—Dylan's (see listing below).
You wouldn't go to Paris and skip the Louvre. Well, you shouldn't come to New York and skip The Met, one of the world's largest and most impressive museums with three million objects on display and incredible art exhibits, including the new Greek and Roman wing. Additionally, kids ages three through seven years old (and their parents) can engage in storytelling, sketching and exploring art on many weekday afternoons and weekend mornings (call for schedule). On **Friday and Saturday evenings**, from 4 to 5pm, kids six to 12 and their parents (or grandparents) can partici-pate in a lecture series that includes sketching. Kids can also get an ac-tivity handout at the front desk in the information lobby.

One of the coolest and most unique things about the Met is the roof

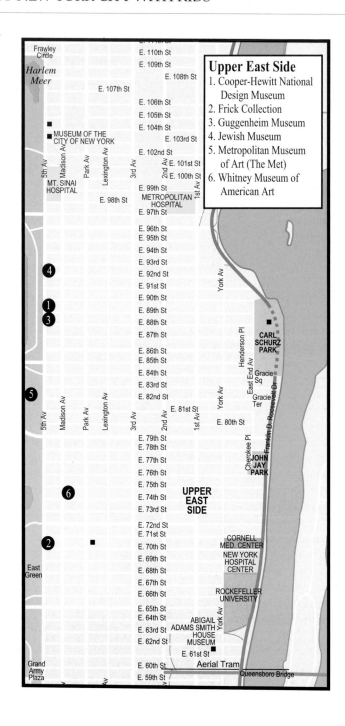

Upper East Side

1. Cooper-Hewitt National Design Museum
2. Frick Collection
3. Guggenheim Museum
4. Jewish Museum
5. Metropolitan Museum of Art (The Met)
6. Whitney Museum of American Art

sculpture garden. The views of Manhattan are super and the scene is low-key. There is a café that serves wraps and other goodies, as well as a bar. Teens will love the virgin pina coladas and strawberry daiquiris; adults will love the wine selection. The striking sculptures will wow the kids—as well as adults. Hey single parents: the Sculpture Roof Garden is apparently a good place to meet other singles.

There are several places to eat in the museum including a cafeteria-style eatery (best bet for families) in the lower level and a more upscale restaurant on the first floor that overlooks Central Park. For coffee and dessert, the café in the American wing is a winner.

Tip: Make sure to get one of the printed *Family Guides* at the Info Desk at the beginning of your visit. There is also a *Family Audio Guide* that features 100 works of art in 10 easy-to-follow, one-hour tours.

Parent Tip

If you visit New York in early June you're in for a cultural treat. For the past 25 years, the city has celebrated a Museum Mile Festival held the second Tuesday in June. Nine of New York's most fabulous Fifth Avenue museums are open to visitors—free of charge. Fifth Avenue from 82nd street to 104th street is closed to traffic for a mile while live bands and street performers join in to celebrate museum day. Also during this much-anticipated event, kids can roll up their sleeves and make art. The activities vary each year but past artsy activities have included map-making at the Museum of the City of New York and chalk painting in the streets.

The Solomon R. Guggenheim Museum

1071 Fifth Avenue (89th Street), Tel. 212/423-3500, www.guggenheim.org.

Open: Saturday through Wednesday 10am to 5:45pm, Friday open until 7:45pm. Closed Thursday.

Admission: $18 adults, $15 seniors and students, kids 12 years old and under are free. Friday is pay-what-you-wish between 5:45pm and 7:45pm.

Subway: 4, 5, 6 (86th Street).

Come to show the kids a beautiful Frank Lloyd Wright piece of architecture—the building itself is stunning. The collection of Picassos, Chagall, van Gogh and other important 20th-century artists competes for adoration. Check the museum's website for current listings of family events and workshops.

The Whitney Museum of American Art

945 Madison Avenue (74th and 75th Streets), 800/944-8639, www.whitney.org.

Open: Wednesday, Thursday, Saturday and Sunday 11am to 6pm, Friday 1pm to 9pm. Closed Monday and Tuesday.

Admission: $15 adults, $10 seniors and students, kids 12 years old and younger are free. Pay what you wish on Friday 6pm to 9pm.

Subway: 6 (77th Street).

Don't let the stark institutional look intimidate you. The Whitney Museum is home to some of the best contemporary American art in the country, including a permanent collection of Edward Hopper, Jasper Johns, Georgia O'Keeffe and Roy Lichtenstein. Tweens and teenagers will appreciate this museum—and parents will enjoy sharing the experience. Be sure to pick up free *Family Guides* in the lobby before viewing. There's also a free *Family Audio Guide* that covers the museum's permanent collection.

Ongoing kids programs include storytelling about the art or a reading of a book by celebrated American authors—kids are encouraged to respond by drawing or sketching. Strollers are allowed in the museum, although not every exhibit. There's a wonderful and popular restaurant here, Sarabeth's, but they don't take reservations and it can get crowded.

The Frick Collection

1 East 70th Street (between Madison and Fifth Avenues), Tel. 212/288-0700, www.frick.org.

Open: Tuesday through Saturday 10am to 6pm, Sunday 11am to 5pm. Closed Monday.

Admission: $15 adults, $10 seniors, $5 students, kids under 10 years old not admitted. Sunday is pay-what-you-wish from 11am to 1pm.

Subway: 6.

If your kids are ten years old or older, your family will enjoy stopping by this gorgeous Gilded Age mansion to see paintings and sculptures from the Renaissance through 19th century (think Rembrandt, Michelangelo and Vermeer). If your kid is an art or architecture lover, it's worth a look (although it isn't a cheap outing). Note: kids 10 and under aren't allowed.

Cooper-Hewitt National Design Museum

Smithsonian Institution, corner of Fifth Avenue and 91st Street, Tel. 212/849-8400, www.si.edu/ndm.

Open: Monday through Thursday 10am to 5pm, Friday 10am to 9pm, Saturday 10am to 6pm, Sunday noon to 6pm. Closed Thanksgiving, Christmas and New Years Day.

Admission: $15 adult; $10 seniors and students with ID; free for kids under twelve years old.

Subway: 4, 5, 6.

The setting for this museum jewel, whose mission is to explore the impact of design in our daily lives, is the landmark Andrew Carnegie mansion. A pretty place to visit if you're in town during a spell of rainy days or frigid temps.

The Jewish Museum

1109 Fifth Avenue (92nd Street), Tel. 212/423-3200, www.thejewishmuseum.org.

Open: Saturday through Wednesday 11am to 5:45pm, Friday closed. Open Thursday until 8pm. Closed Jewish holidays.

Admission: $12 adults, $10 seniors and students, kids 12 years old and younger are free. Free on Saturdays. Thursday is pay-what-you-wish between 5pm and 8pm.

Subway: 4, 5, 6.

"Not another museum," your kids are sure to say (*see photo on next page*). Visit here on **Family Fun Sundays** (every Sunday, except on Jewish holidays, September through May) and they'll have faith that this isn't a boring museum. Dedicated to Jewish art and culture, this lovely museum features a Drop-In Arts and Crafts in the Activity Center from 1pm to 4pm for kids three and older. Ongoing arts projects that relate

Parent Tip

Satisfy your sweet tooth at Dylan's Candy Bar, an outrageous—and pricey—candy store that's owned by Ralph Lauren's daughter, Dylan. This dentist's dream is eye candy, too—towering rows of colorful candies bring a smile. In fact, there are 5,000 varieties of candies here. Note: The days of penny candy are history and Dylan's will cost you. Bonus: Sit on one of the peppermint-shaped stools at the Dessert Café and Chocolate Bar to enjoy hot fudge sundaes that are made with real, oozing hot fudge. My son is a hot fudge sundae freak and he gives first prize to Dylan's. Located at 1011 Third Avenue (at 60th Street), 646/735-0078, www.dylanscandybar.com. Open: Monday through Thursday 10am to 9pm, Friday and Saturday 10am to 11pm and Sunday 11am to 8pm.

to the museum's permanent collection, a Jewish holiday or special exhibition engage the kids. There are also **Family Gallery Talks** on Sundays—guided tours of the galleries that are led by the museum's junior docents. Sketching in the Galleries is another exciting program for 5 to 12 year olds (free with museum admission). For really young ones (2 to 5 years old), story time is sweet (free with museum admission). There is a new children's exhibition called *Archaeology Zone: Discovering Treasures from Playgrounds to Palaces*. Bonus: Café Weissman serves kosher cuisine.

The Museum of the City of New York

1220 Fifth Avenue (at 103rd Street), 212/534-1672, www.mcny.org.

Open: Tuesday through Sunday 10am to5pm. Closed Mondays.

Admission: Suggested admission—$9 adults, $5 seniors and students, $20 families. Admission is free on Sundays between 10am and noon.

Subway: 6,2,3

Explore all things New York at this exciting uptown space that also features family programs like an Earth Day workshop.

9. UPPER WEST SIDE

The Upper West Side is home to one of the best kid-friendly museums in the world—the American Museum of Natural History (*see photo below*)—as well as Lincoln Center, the Time Warner Center, and lots of great restaurants, movie theaters and the much-celebrated Zabar's.

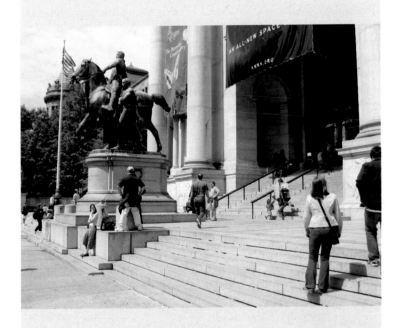

American Museum of Natural History

Central Park West (at 79th Street), Tel. 212/769-5100. www.amnh.org.

Open: Daily 10am to 5:45pm, The Rose Center is open late on the first Friday of every month until 8:45pm (Closed Thanksgiving and Christmas).

Admission: There are several admission policies. The museum has a suggested donation policy. Admission to the Museum and Rose Center is $15 adults, $8.50 kids ages 2 to 12 years old, and $11 seniors and students. Admission to the shows at the Hayden Planetarium (and the Rose Center and the museum) are $30 adults, $19 kids (ages 2 to 12 years old), seniors/students $23.

Subway: 1, B, C.

If your kids have patience for only one museum while visiting the City, this is the one (hopefully, though, you'll have time to take in the Metropolitan Museum of Art, as well.) The American Museum of Natural History is pleasing to kids as well as adults, with more than 45 permanent exhibition halls and special exhibitions, **IMAX films**, Space Shows at the **Hayden Planetarium** and the stunning **Rose Center for Earth and Space.** In the museum itself, there is a handful of exhibit halls, including the Hall of Biodiversity (rainforest diorama); Culture Hall, dedicated to anthropology; Mammals Hall (think dioramas of mammals); Hall of African Mammals; the ever-popular Fossil Halls (including two dinosaur exhibit halls that tell the story through the evolutionary process rather than chronological age); and the Milstein Hall of Ocean Life (home to the very popular 94-foot-long model of a blue whale). New is a display of mineral specimens in the Guggenheim Hall of Minerals.

Hands-down favorites of most kids, including my son: the Blue Whale and the dinosaur fossils. Dioramas are cool if you look and move on, but don't expect your kids to want to linger too long at these exhibits. Kids will

be happy to hang out by the dinos and whale all day, though.

You can take an hour-long tour to see five of the halls led by a museum guide (included in the price of admission). Or, spend the day exploring on your own.

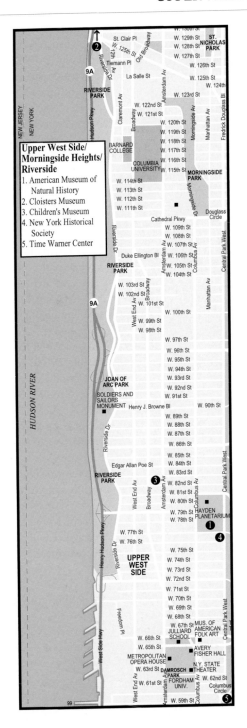

**Upper West Side/
Morningside Heights/
Riverside**

1. American Museum of
   Natural History
2. Cloisters Museum
3. Children's Museum
4. New York Historical
   Society
5. Time Warner Center

Parent Tip

If any of your children love to dance—tap, ballet, modern—*sashay* your way over to Steps, an incredible dance school on the Upper West Side. Take the tiny elevator to the nine studios on the upper floors (large windows allow lots of light to flood in) and watch some of New York's best dancers—as well as amateurs—*plie*, tap and lunge. I spent many hours here taking dance classes at Steps. Your ballerina girl or Mishawannabe might be inspired to sign up for a class—go for it. It doesn't get any cooler than to take a dance class in a hip Manhattan dance studio. Wait 'til they tell their friends back home! Steps offers 50 open classes a day; sign up in person at the desk. Located at 2121 Broadway (at 74th Street), Tel. 212/874-2410, www.stepsnyc.com.

The icing on the cake at the museum is the Rose Center for Earth and Space; the Space Shows take the prize. They rotate but at press time they included *SonicVision: How Do You Hear Your Music*, a digitally animated alternative music show. And *The Search for Life: Are We Alone?*. The featured film is *Cosmic Collisions*, a journey into deep space, narrated by Robert Redford.

Bonus: Come for Starry Nights with Live Jazz the first Friday night of every month (tapas, wine, beverages).

IMAX films are another museum highlight. At press time *"Dinosaurs Alive"* was being shown. You'll have to pay extra for the IMAX movie, but your ticket will also get you into the Rose Center and the museum. IMAX ticket prices fluctuate depending on the film; check the website or call for up-to-date information.

There are also tons of family programs and workshops that take place year-round (visit the website or phone the museum for up-to-date information).

When stomachs start rumbling, the pickings used to be slim at the Museum just several years back. That's changed. There's a food court on the lower level (sandwiches, pizza, barbecue, salad bar.)

Children's Museum of Manhattan
    212 West 83rd Street (between Broadway and Amsterdam), Tel. 212/721-1234, www.cmom.org.
    Open: Tuesday through Sunday 10am to 5pm. Closed Monday.
    Admission: $9 adults, $6 seniors, kids under 1 years old free. Free admission 5pm to 8pm 1st Friday of the month.
    Subway: 1, B, C.

Food for Thought on the Upper West Side

Here are two great food tips:

• When my son was an infant we lived directly across the street from Café Lalo on West 83rd Street (the Children's Museum is located a couple doors down), a sweet café with frothy cappuccinos in a setting of exposed brick walls and floor-to-ceiling windows. But the best thing about this neighborhood spot—and Hollywood set (Meg Ryan and Tom Hank's *You've Got Mail* was filmed here)—was the ceiling fans. My son was completely mesmerized by the gently whirling fans. I'd strategically sit at a table that had a primo ceiling fan view for Alex and then I'd actually *enjoy* my cup of foamy cappucino and conversation with a friend or good book.

Even if the fans aren't whirling, Café Lalo has many fans. It's a great spot for coffee and dessert (choose from more than 150 gourmet desserts). And Café Lalo also does brunch (organic cereals, steamed eggs, smoked fish, salads, Belgian waffles) from 8 am and 4 pm weekdays and between 9 am and 4 pm on weekends. Open: Monday through Thursday 8 am to 2 am, Friday 8 am to 4 am and Sunday 9 am to 2 am. Visit www.cafelalo.com

• You haven't been to the Upper West Side if you haven't visited Zabar's, a sensational food store and New York landmark. Forty thousand people a week shop here, hitting the who-knew-there-were-that-many-types-of-cheese department, the fresh fish and caviar section, and the bakery where fresh croissants march out of the ovens. Zabar's has a special place in the hearts of New Yorkers who walk, take subways and buses to shop here every week. Bonus: Visit Zabar's and then head east a couple of blocks to Central Park to find a swath of lawn and call it a picnic! We did this often. Open 365 days a year, Monday through Friday 8 am to 7:30 pm; Saturday 8 am to 8 pm; Sunday 9 am to 6 pm. Located at: 2245 Broadway (at 80th Street), Tel. 212/787-2000 or visit www.zabars.com.

This five-floor museum is tucked into a neighborhood street on the Upper West Side (*see photo below*). We lived next door to this museum and I can tell you it's a busy place with New York families on weekends, nannies with young children and school groups on weekdays and, of course, tourists. The museum can get crowded, especially on rainy days and during school holidays. Keep in mind that the museum's exhibits are skewed to younger kids, eight years old and under, with tons of interactive things for them to do, especially *really* young kids. The Playworks (for one month olds to four year olds) stimulates learning in babies and pre-schoolers, and the Early Childhood Center (for kids 18 months to 4 years old) is a safe bet for kids who love to explore, climb, slide, paint and sing. Older kids like the interactive "TV Station" and Computer Lab. In the summer, the outdoor **CitySplash** is a hit. A new exhibit is *Gods, Myths and Morals: Discover Ancient Greece*—kids can a climb huge Trojan horse.

New York Historical Society
170 Central Park West, Tel. 212/873-3400, www.nyhistory.org.
Open: Tuesday through Saturday 10am to 6pm, Sunday 11am to 5:45pm, Friday open until 8pm. Closed Monday.
Admission: $10 adults, $7 seniors, $6 students, free for kids 12 and under. Budget Tip: Free admission on Fridays from 6pm to 8pm.
Subway: B, C.

If your kids are history buffs this museum will hold their interest with exhibits that include artifacts from the Civil War and the 18th century. Bonus: The Café at N-YHS here is catered by Zabars.

The Time Warner Center Columbus Circle
Columbus Circle.
Subway: 1, 2, 3, A, C, B, D

Home to one of New York's most expensive hotels (The Mandarin Oriental; see separate listing in our hotel chapter), as well as a collection of upscale restaurants and boutiques, the Time Warner Center is a welcome addition to what was once a part of town that was an eyesore.

10. CENTRAL PARK

New York's jewel, **Central Park** is a giant playground for kids and adults, rich and poor, as well as a perennial favorite spot for tourists to visit. Of course, the warm weather months are especially great times to hang, stroll, roller blade, jog, bicycle and picnic in the Park. But most New Yorkers love to play in the Park year-round. Word to the wise: The park is not a place to hang after the sun has set, unless of course, it's summertime and you are attending one of the fabulous concerts or a Shakespeare play.

If you love to jog or run, lace up your running shoes and hit the **Reservoir**, a 1.58-mile dirt path that's been renamed the Jacqueline Kennedy Onassis Reservoir in recent years (it was a favorite spot of the former First Lady.) I used to run here after work every day (if the sun hadn't yet set.) Even if you aren't a runner, a stroll around the reservoir is enjoyable and the views of the Manhattan skyline are great. There are tons of kid-friendly things in the Park, including the fabulous **Zoo** and fun-loving **Carousel**.

Because Central Park is so expansive, there are a number of subway lines and stations that serve it. They are:

- **West Side:**

    A, C, B, D, 1 to 59th Street station

    B, C to 72nd Street station, 81st Street station and 86th Street station

- **East Side:**

    N, R to 5th Avenue station

    6 to 68th Street station, 77th Street station, 86th Street station, 96th Street station, 103rd Street station and 110th Street station

Belvedere Castle/Henry Luce Observatory

Located mid-park at 79th Street, Tel. 212/772-0210, www.centralpark.org.

Open: Tuesday through Sunday 10am to 5pm.

Sitting pretty on Vista Rock, Belvedere Castle is the second highest natural elevation in the Park. In Italian, Belvedere means "panaromic viewpoint," and the views from the Castle are stunners. The Castle had suffered from years of neglect and vandalism until 1983 when it was rescued and restored by the Central Park Conservancy. Tip: Visit the Official Weather Center on the 2nd floor; weather data has been collected here since 1919.

The Central Park Wildlife Conservation Society's Zoo and Children's Zoo

839 Fifth Avenue (between 63rd and 66th streets), Tel. 212/439-6500, www.centralpark.com.

Open: April through October, Monday through Friday 10am to 5pm, Saturday and Sunday 10am to 5:30pm and holidays 10am to 5:30pm. November through March, 10am to 4:30pm daily.

Admission: Daily, $8 adults, kids 3 to 12 years old $3, seniors (65 years and older) $4.

The beauty of this zoo is that it's so easy to get to, thanks to its location just steps from Fifth Avenue in Central Park. The zoo is home to more than 1,400 animals of more than 130 species.

My son and my nephews' favorite zoo activities include the feeding of the seals in the sea lion pool. Feeding time is 11:30am, 2pm and 4pm. Also a kick is the penguin feeding at 10:30am and 2:30pm. The polar bear exhibit is also really cool. The Tisch Children's Zoo here is especially popular with the diaper crowd. Goats, sheep, a cow and a Vietnamese potbellied pig will tug at the littlest ones' hearts. Kids can feed these animals (you can buy a handful of food for 25 cents from a dispenser). Kids also giggle when they "pet" the bronze animal sculptures that are located next to each pen and a squeak or squawk is emitted. The **Enchanted Forest** is centrally located in the Zoo. There is an aviary with live turtles, frogs and birds and a children's theater (there are two theaters in the Zoo, the other is located in the central courtyard.) Daily shows about animals are performed daily for kids.

And don't miss the **George Delacorte Musical Clock**, located between the Wildlife Center and the Children's Zoo. Every hour on the hour and every half-hour one of 32 nursery rhyme tunes plays while a bear with tambourine, a hippopotamus with violin, a goat with pan pipes, a kangaroo and offspring with horns, and a penguin with drum parade around the base of the clock. The animals give a shorter performance on the half-hour. (There are also appropriately played seasonal tunes throughout the year).

Bonus: Take a free tour led by wildlife guides, every Tuesday at 2:30pm. The tour meets at the penguin exhibit. Note: Advance reservations are required; call the number above.

Another bonus: If your kids are nocturnal like mine (my son thinks sleep is a complete waste of time), why not join the other nocturnal creatures at the Central Park Zoo on an **overnight sleepover.** Yep, you sleep inside the zoo! Snooze at the Zoo is offered three times a year between October and February. The program is educationally skewed: kids make crafts, learn about some of the animal habitats and watch the zookeepers at work preparing the animal's breakfast. Cost: $160 each adult/child pairing. For more information or to make reservations, call 212/459-6583.

The Harlem Meer

106th to 110th eastside, Tel. 212/ 860-1370, www.centralparknyc.org.

This lovely body of water (*meer* is Dutch for "lake") in the upper northern reaches of the Park has been restored to become a spectacular, rugged setting. The 11-acre meer is stocked with bass, catfish, shiners and bluegills. One of the most popular things for families (kids and adults) here is the catch-and-release fishing program. The Dana Discovery Center (see next entry) supplies the poles, unbarbed hooks (remember, this is a catch-and-release program) and instruction booklets. Bonuses: Two playgrounds with cool water features. Come at Halloween for the pumpkin sail of candlelit Jack o' Lanterns across the meer.

Shakespeare in the Park

It doesn't get any better than this for kids who love the theater. For the last 50 years, Shakespeare in the Park has offered Broadway-quality Shakespeare performances throughout the summer at Central Park's Delacorte Theater—for free. Tickets are required and are distributed on the day of the performance at the Delacorte Theater at 1pm and at the Public Theater (425 Lafayette Street) between 1pm and 3pm. Performances are given Tuesday through Sunday at 8:30pm late May through mid-August. Caveat: These are hard tickets to come by. Tips: It's easier to snag tickets earlier in the season, and you should arrive early to wait in line before the 1pm distribution of tickets begins. For more information, visit www.publictheater.org.

The Charles A. Dana Discovery Center

Located at 110th Street and Lenox Avenue inside the Park, on the northern shore of the Harlem Meer, Tel. 212/860-1370, www.centralparknyc.org.

Open: Tuesday through Sunday 10am to 5pm.

Central Park's newest building, which opened in 1993, is one of four visitor centers in the Park; this one serves Upper Park visitors. It's also the place for the Central Park Conservancy's free family and community events. The Great Hall here, host to collaborative exhibits with City museums and other institutions, has a small deck that overlooks the Meer and views of the Park's southern environs. Bonus: Jazz concerts and other performance festivals and fun events are also staged here.

The Loeb Boathouse

Located on the East Side between 74th and 75th Streets, 212/517-2233, www.centralparknyc.org.

Rowboat rentals: March through October, daily 10am to 5pm (weather permitting). Cost: $12 first hour and $3 each additional 15 minutes (a $30 cash deposit is required).

Bicycle Rentals: Cost: $9 to $15 per hour (credit card, driver's license or passport required).

Gondola rides: In the summer Monday through Friday 5pm to 9pm and Saturday and Sunday 2pm to 9pm. Cost: $30 per half-hour.

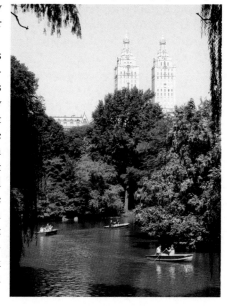

A favorite spot of adults and children, this is the unspoken central headquarters of the park. There are many things you can do here: Rent rowboats (up to five people per boat) or take a Venetian gondola ride on the lake. Rent bicycles at the bicycle rental concession for a spin in the park. Enjoy some snacks on the outside terrace or dine at the restaurant, which overlooks the lake and has a deck with overhead heating so you can sit outside.

Parent Tip

You don't necessarily have to travel to Yankee or Shea stadiums to take in a ball game and hot dogs. The New York Gotham Baseball Club reenacts games played the way they were in 1864 on the Great Lawn in Central Park throughout the summer. Remember, New York City is where the game was invented (well, that's one theory anyway). For a game schedule and more info go to www.zyworld.com/gothambaseball. Tip: There are dozens of hot dog vendors throughout the park.

The Ramble

Located mid-park from 73rd to 79th streets, to the west of the entrance of the Boathouse, www.centralparknyc.org.

New Yorkers love this 3.8 acre totally artificial "wild garden" that was created (only the bedrock existed, everything else was made). Twenty-six species of butterflies make their home here, as well as 320 bird species. There's a tumbling stream called "The Gill." Note: There are sections that are fenced off as part of efforts to preserve the land.

Conservatory Garden

Located mid-park from 104th to 106th streets on the east side (enter at Fifth Avenue and 105th street or at the 106th street gate inside the Park. Open: 8am to dusk.

A lovely, six-acre formal garden that takes its name from the glass conservatory that once stood here. There are actually three separate gardens, each representing different styles: Italian, French and English. The gardens features bronze sculptures, fountains and, of course, shrubs and flowers.

Sheep Meadow

Located on the west side, mid-park between 66th and 69th streets.

Open: May to mid-October, 11am to dusk (weather permitting).

New Yorkers love this giant—15 acres—grassy space. If the sun is

shining and the temps are warm, this expanse of velvet green is spot on for sunbathing and picnics. Bonus: Lilac Walk, on the northern edge of Sheep Meadow, features 23 different varieties of lilacs from around the globe. A much-revered slice of paradise in a concrete jungle of a city.

Strawberry Fields

Located on the west side between 71st and 74th streets.

This teardrop shaped piece of land honors John Lennon of the Beatles, who was killed across the street in front of his apartment building, the Dakota (72nd street and Central Park West). Strawberry Fields is named after the Beatles song *Strawberry Fields Forever*. Lennon's wife, Yoko Ono, donated $1 million to the Central Park Conservancy to landscape and maintain the park and countries from all over the globe donated trees.

Whenever we come here there is always at least one person playing guitar while sitting near the black-and-white mosaic design which reads IMAGINE, the title of one of Lennon's songs. Often, there is impromptu singing of Beatles songs by visitors who also light candles and place flowers on the mosaic as a tribute to Lennon. It's a quiet, reflective and humbling spot in the middle of a bustling city that Lennon adored. When George Harrison died, Strawberry Fields was packed with Beatles' fans who gathered to sing and reflect.

As you stroll this peaceful part of the park, you'll come across a bronze plaque that lists the 121 countries that endorse Strawberry Fields as a Garden of Peace.

The Dairy

Located mid-park at 65th Street, Tel. 212/794-6564.

Open: Tuesday through Sunday 10am to 5pm.

In the 19th century, children would be rewarded in the Park with a glass of fresh milk from this quirky Victorian building. One side of the building is an open loggia, made of wood with geometric gingerbread trim. The other side is made of granite with spires reminiscent of a country church. The view from the Dairy is quintessential New York: Wollman Rink with the skyline as a backdrop.

Parent Tip

A popular way to see Central Park year-round is by horse-drawn carriage. I feel sorry for the horses who jockey for space with cabs and other traffic. But these rides are enormously popular with romantics and families alike. You'll see the carriages lined up at the southern end of the Park along Central Park South (beginning at 59th Street, across from FAO Schwarz and the Plaza Hotel) between Fifth and Sixth avenues. Cost: $34 for the first 20 minutes and $54 for a 45 to 50 minute tour. Call 212/736-0680 for more information.

• The Ballfields Café, just west of the carousel near 66th street, is the perfect spot to stop for a bit before or after taking a spin on the Carousel. Think PBJ, hot dogs and al fresco seating.

• The Central Park Conservancy offers many free programs throughout the year for kids of all ages. For an up-to-date listing go to the Central Park Conservancy's website at www.centralparknyc.org. Note: You must register for these events.

You can't get a glass of milk here any longer though. Today, the building houses a Visitor Center where you can pick up brochures and maps and gather information about the history of Central Park, as well as events that are taking place in the Park. The Dairy is also the Park's official gift shop.

Look west of the Dairy and you'll spy what is called "children's mountain," a large bedrock outcrop on which the brick **Chess and Checkers House** stands. There are 24 shaded chess tables and players come from all over to play here.

Carousel

Located mid-park at 64th Street, Tel. 212/879-0244.

Open: Daily April through November 10am to 6pm, weekends November through April open 10am to 4:30pm. Cost: $1.25 per ride.

No trip to Manhattan with kids is complete without a spin on this vintage carousel, one of the largest carousels in the country with 58 hand-carved painted horses. Makes for sweet memories.

The Great Lawn

Located mid-park from 79th to 85th streets.

Eureka! If you are visiting the City in the summer, you must take in one of the City's most treasured pleasures: an evening concert by the **New York Philharmonic** or the **Metropolitan Opera**, each of which performs twice. The performances complement the Manhattan skyline views for an evening of New York magic. You'll share this 55-acre Crayola green swath of lawn with about a million New Yorkers, so it's best to stake out your blanket territory early in the day. You won't be alone. New Yorkers are very territorial and many arrive at dawn to stake their claim. New Yorkers also know how to plan a gourmet picnic—you won't believe some of the elaborate spreads: champagne, pates, lobster, candelabras…. You certainly won't want to look like a tourist so plan to bring a picnic yourselves.

Your best bet for picnic fare are: Visit Zabar's on the Upper West Side to create your own picnic (*see sidebar on page 73*).

Alice in Wonderland Statue

Located East 74th Street, north of the Conservatory Water.

Little girls especially love to pay a visit to Alice and her entourage from the Lewis Carroll classic *Alice's Adventures in Wonderland*. There's the Mad Hatter, the March Hare, and the Cheshire Cat. The sculpture by Jose de Creeft was commissioned by philanthropist George Delacorte to honor his wife, Margarita. Kids aren't drawn to the sculpture as much to admire it as to climb and explore its many surfaces and textures (*see photo below*).

Bethesda Fountain

Located mid-park at 72nd Street.

This fountain is a great meeting spot, as well as a perfect spot to while away some down time. An angel adorns the fountain's center. And there's usually always someone strumming a guitar or humming a harmonica.

Swedish Cottage Marionette Theatre

Located on the west side at 79th Street, you must make reservations, Tel. 212/988-9093.

Show times: Tuesday through Friday 10:30am and noon, Saturdays and Sundays 1pm. Closed Mondays and school and national holidays.

Admission: $6 adults, $5 children.

Jack in the Beanstalk, Cinderella and *Hansel and Gretel* are part of the repertoire of the marionette theater company that performs here. They write or adapt their own scripts, as well as construct and costume the puppets. They recently performed a new interpretation of *Pippi Longstocking*. Productions rotate so call to see what will be playing when you are visiting.

11. THE OUTER BOROUGHS

There is plenty of cool stuff for the kids outside of Manhattan: **Queens** features Shea Stadium, where the Mets play, the Queens Zoo, and the New York Hall of Science; the **Bronx** has the one and only Yankee Stadium and the Cloisters Museum, a wonderful respite from the hustle and bustle of everyday life; in **Brooklyn**, children of all ages will love the New York Aquarium and the beautiful Botanic Garden (*photo below*); and in Staten Island the main attraction is the Children's Museum.

QUEENS

Flushing Meadows Corona Park
Long Island Expressway (Roosevelt Avenue Van Wyck Expressway—111th Street), Tel. 718/760-6562 www.flushingmeadowscoronapark.org.
Open: Seven days 10am to 5pm, all year round.
Subway: No. 7 to 111th Street or Willets Point/Shea Stadium.
Train: Long Island Rail Road (LIRR).

This enormous 1,255-acre park, which once hosted the 1939 and 1964 World's Fair is home to many attractions, including an art museum, a science museum, a botanical garden, a baseball stadium, two lakes (one accessible), a miniature golf course and a pitch-and-putt golf course (see golf listings). The park's centerpiece is the Unisphere, a 140-foot-tall, stainless steel ball that was presented to the 1964 World's Fair by U.S. Steel. You can picnic and play in the park (see parks listings) or, visit the following attractions.

Queens Museum of Art
Flushing Meadows Corona Park, Tel. 718/592-9700, www.queensmuseum.org.
Open: Wednesday through Friday 10am to 5pm, Saturday and Sunday noon to 5pm. Closed major holidays.
Admission: (suggested donation) $5 adults, $2.50 seniors and kids, children five years old and under are free.
Subway: 7 to Willets Point/Shea Stadium.
Train: LIRR.

The main reason you'll want to visit this museum: The **Panorama of the City of New York**, the world's largest architectural scale model, is really cool for kids. Originally constructed for the 1964 World's Fair, this 9,335-square-foot replica of New York City includes more than 900,000 buildings. This is a mind-boggling exhibit for kids. Note: The museum will undergo an ambitious expansion project and when it reopens in 2010 it will be double in size.

The Queens Botanical Garden
43-50 Main Street, Flushing, Tel. 718/886-3800, www.queensbotanical.org.
Open: Spring/summer hours April through October Tuesday through Friday 8am to 6pm and Saturday and Sunday 8am to 7pm. November

through March Tuesday through Saturday 8am to 4:30pm. Closed Mondays.

Admission: Free (donations are welcome).

Subway/Train: 7 subway or Long Island Rail Road/ Port Washington line to Main Street-Flushing. Take the Q44 bus or walk south 8 blocks.

A pretty All-America Trial Garden (displays of annual flowers and vegetables) is one reason to visit the 39-acre garden as is the Fragrant Walk. Another reason: the price is right.

New York Hall of Science

47-01 111th Street (at 48th Avenue), Flushing Meadows-Corona Park, Tel. 718/699-0005, www.nyscience.org.

Open: Summer hours—Monday through Friday 9:30am to 5pm, Saturday and Sunday 10am to 6pm. Fall/Winter/Spring hours—Tuesday through Thursday 9:30am to 2pm, Friday 9:30am to 5pm, Saturday and Sunday noon to 6pm Closed Mondays except holidays. Note: There are special winter holiday hours.

Admission: Adults (ages 18 years old and older) $11 children (2 to 17 years old, college with ID) $8, kids two and under are free. Senior citizens (ages 62 and older) $8. Note: Free admission is offered Fridays between 2 and 5pm and Sundays between 10am and 11am (September 1 through June 30). Note: No free hours during the summer months. Science playground fees: $3 per person, $2 for group (the playground is open March through December, weather permitting, to children of all ages with adult supervision). Strollers are permitted.

Subway: 7 to 111th Street, then walk three blocks south.

Slides, seesaws, more than two-dozen playground elements—with an educational bent (gravity, motion, etc.)—attract kids to the indoor-outdoor **Science Playground** here. There are more than 400 hands-on exhibits, and deftly-performed cool science demonstrations throughout this Queens museum. Exhibits include teen-friendly stuff like the Sports Challenge where kids test their skills at interactive sports like basketball, tennis, and surfing and then see how they can improve by applying the laws of science. There's also an interactive math exhibit and a preschool place.

Bonus: There is a new café onsite—you can eat outdoors on the patio during the nice weather or indoors when the weather is bad.

The Queens Zoo

53-51 111th Street at 53rd Avenue, Flushing Meadows Corona Park. Tel. 718/271-1500, www.nyzoosandaquarium.org.

Open: Monday through Friday 10am to 5pm, Saturday and Sunday 10am to 5:30pm, holidays 10am to 5:30pm (open 365 days a year). Winter hours: the zoo closes at 4:30pm.

Admission: Adults $6, kids (3 to 12) $2, seniors (65 years and older) $2.25.

Subway: 7 to 111th Street, then walk a couple of blocks south to 46th Avenue.

More than 400 animals call this 11-acre zoo home sweet home. If you're really into zoos and have time to check out all of the zoos in the area, pay a visit. Otherwise stick with the Central Park Zoo or Bronx Zoo.

The American Museum of the Moving Image

35th Avenue at 36th Street, Astoria, Tel. 718/784-0077, www.ammi.org.

Open: Wednesday, Thursday noon to 5pm, Friday 11am to 8pm, Saturday and Sunday 11am to 6:30pm. Friday through Sunday there are extended hours for screenings. Closed Mondays (except holidays) and Tuesday.

Admission: $10 adults, $7.50 seniors and students, $5 kids between five years old and 18 years old. Free admission on Friday after 4pm.

Subway: N, W, R, G.

Kids who love television and the movies will enjoy this museum that houses a collection of costumes, cameras and props. The museum is also hands-on for kids interested in the movie making process. It also screens movies and is the site for celebrity-studded events. **Bonus:** Vintage video arcade games like Donkey Kong that visitors can play.

Queens County Farm Museum

73-50 Little Neck Pkwy (Union Turnpike and Grand Central Parkway), Floral Park, Queens, Tel. 718/347-FARM, www.queensfarm.org.

Open: Monday through Friday 9am to 5pm, year-round (outdoor visiting only); and Saturday and Sunday 10am to 5pm tours of the historic farmhouse are given.

Admission: Free.

Subway: E or F train to Kew Gardens/Union Tpke Station or take the Port Washington branch on the Long Island Rail Road (LIRR) to Little Neck Station.

A working historical farm that's a short-term diversion for kids—if you're in the neighborhood. Otherwise, opt for the Central Park or Bronx zoos. **Bonus:** It's a free attraction.

Shea Stadium
126th Street & Roosevelt Avenue, Flushing, Queens, Tel. 718/507-8499, www.mets.com.

Subway: It's easy to get to the Stadium from Manhattan. By subway, take the #7 train to Willets Point/Shea Stadium. It's a quick five-minute walk from the station to the stadium. You can also take the Long Island Rail Road from Penn Station; take the Port Washington line (this line makes stops at Shea on game days only.)

Shea will soon be history and CitiField will take its place beginning with the 2009 season. This ballpark that's home to the Mets hasn't had the same allure as its rival stadium in the Bronx (Mets fans may take exception to my saying so). Still, the ball club is beloved by millions of New Yorkers and Long Islanders and packs 'em in for games. If you're in town for one of the "subway series" games between the Yankees and Mets, you'll see Shea Stadium filled to the rafters. Originally, the stadium was to be called Flushing Meadow Park, thanks to its location in Flushing Meadows-Corona Park. But the stadium was renamed as a tribute to William Shea, the gentleman who was responsible for bringing the National League back to the City. A fun-loving, New York baseball stadium.

Parent Tip

If the Mets are in town and you want to see a day game, combine a visit to Shea Stadium with a visit to one of the Flushing Meadows-Corona Park attractions listed above. It's easy to do. You'll take the Number 7 train to the Shea Stadium stop—the subway stop for both Shea and Flushing Meadows. Note: The same tip applies if you are visiting around Labor Day when the U.S. Open is at the Billie Jean King National Tennis Center, a baseball throw away from Shea Stadium and the Park's exhibits.

Socrates Sculpture Park
Broadway at Vernon Blvd., Long Island City, Tel. 718/956-1819,
www.socratessculpturepark.org.
Open: 10am to sunset year-round.
Admission: Free.
Subway: N or W Train to Broadway stop in Queens, then walk eight
blocks toward the East River.

Queens' residents are very proud of this park and outdoor museum,
which they adore for its contemporary sculpture and East River views.
Bonus: Kids can climb the structures. If you are visiting in June, the
Summer Solstice Festival is special, with storytelling and face painting for
children. Also in the summer is a free, weekly outdoor cinema series in
conjunction with the Museum of Moving Image but the movies won't hold
the interest of young kids, better for teens.

STATEN ISLAND

Staten Island Children's Museum
1000 Richmond Terrace, Snug Harbor Cultural Center, Tel. 718/
273-2060, www.statenislandkids.org.
Open: Tuesday through Sunday noon to 5pm; 11am to 5pm during
the summer. Closed Monday.
Admission: $5 adults and kids, free for kids two years old and under.
Free admission for grandparents on Wednesdays.
Getting There: Take the Staten Island ferry and then board the S40
bus to Richmond Terrace.

There is a handful of exhibits at this small museum with some cool
stuff for little tykes like water play and bugs. Kids can also play dress-up in
Portia's Playhouse. You'll especially appreciate the lovely setting at the
Snug Harbor Cultural Center with picnic tables that beckon picnickers.
New exhibit in spring 2008: *House: About It.*

Staten Island Zoo
614 Broadway, Staten Island, Tel. 718/442-3100,
www.statenislandzoo.org.
Open: Daily 10am to 4:45pm.
Admission: $7 adults (15 years and older), $5 seniors, $4 children (3-
to 14 years old), free kids three-years-old and under. Pay-what-you-wish
day is Wednesday after 2pm.

Getting There: Take the Staten Island Ferry (free) to the St. George ferry Terminal where you'll board the S48 bus to Forest Avenue and Broadway. Make a left on Broadway and continue walking a few blocks until you spy the zoo's entrance.

Teeny compared to the rambling Bronx Zoo (and less crowded than the Central Park Zoo), this eight-acre zoo isn't about elephants and rhinos. Instead, it is home to monkeys, snakes, lizards, leopards and antelope and other similarly-sized animals on the survival-of-the-fittest spectrum. A new Africa exhibit recently opened. Also popular are a rainforest and a new reptile wing. Still, if you want to see just one zoo while in the City, opt for the Central Park Zoo or Bronx Zoo.

BROOKLYN

Brooklyn Botanic Garden

1000 Washington Avenue (across from Prospect Park), Tel. 718/623-7200, www.bbg.org.

Open: Mid-March through October Tuesday through Friday 8am to 6pm; weekends and holidays 10am to 6pm; closed Mondays (except holidays that fall on Mondays, but not Labor Day). November through mid-March Tuesday through Friday 8am to 4:30pm; weekends and holidays 10am to 4:30pm. Closed Monday, Thanksgiving, Christmas and New Year's Day (open Mondays that fall on a holiday).

Admission: $8 seniors, $4 students, $4 kids 12 years old and older, kids under 12 years old are free. Note: Admission is free Saturday 10am to noon and all day Tuesday; seniors are free Fridays, too. Admission is free on weekdays late November through February.

Subway: Q train to Prospect Park Station (note: the B train doesn't run on weekends) or the 2 or 3 train to Eastern Parkway.

A 52-acre jewel in Brooklyn—with a twist. There's the sweet fragrance garden for the blind. And a celebrity path with the names of famous Brooklynites: think Woody Allen and Mae West. **Daffodil Hill** is awash in yellow each spring followed closely by a brushstroke of pink when the cherry blossoms that ring the **Japanese Hill and Pond Garden** explode with color. The **Cranford Rose Garden** bursts into bloom early each summer, and when the gardens are frosted in white come winter, you can visit the indoor **Steinhardt Conservatory**, a showplace for orchids. Kids can see how green their thumbs are at the **Discovery Garden**, a 13,000-square-foot center designed for budding botanists with hands-on play activities. Kid's workshops are also offered on weekends. There is also a children's garden.

New York Aquarium at Coney Island
Surf Avenue (and West 8th Street), Brooklyn, Tel. 718/265-FISH, www.nyaquarium.com.
Open: Daily 10am to 5pm in the winter, open until 7pm in the summer. Open 365 days a year. Note: Hours tend to vary seasonally so call or visit the website for updates.

Admission: $12 adults, $8 seniors and kids, kids two years old and younger are free.

Subway: D train to Stillwell Avenue Station in Coney Island.

The daily sea lion shows are worth the price of admission alone. You'll also fall in love with the walruses. All told, there are 300 species of sea life in this 14-acre aquarium. My son's Greenwich Village camp took a field trip here and it was one of the highlights of his summer. Translation: Expect lots of camp groups to share the space in the summer during your visit. Bonus: Submarine ride to the Deep Sea 3-D ride, April through October, 10:30am to 8pm, extra cost.

Brooklyn Children's Museum
145 Brooklyn Avenue (at St. Marks Avenue), Brooklyn, Tel. 718/735-4400, www.bchildmus.org.
Open: At press time, the museum was closed for expansion and was expected to reopen in spring 2008. When it opens, the museum will double in size to 102,000 square feet and will be the first "green" children's museum in the country with roof panels that will generate some of its electricity and a geothermal system of heat pumps and wells to heat and cool the building. The museum will feature a huge space for an early-learning toddler program with child-powered vehicles and water activities.

New York Transit Museum

Corner of Boerum Place and Schermerhorn Street in Brooklyn Heights, Tel. 718/694-1600, www.mta.nyc.ny.us/mta/museum.

Open: Tuesday through Friday 10am to 4pm, Saturday through Sunday noon to 5pm, closed Monday and holidays.

Admission: $5 adults, $3 seniors and kids three years to 17 years old.

Subway: A, C, G, F.

Many kids love trains—my son was obsessed with them when he was real young. This museum, the largest in the country devoted to urban public transportation history, has been renovated in recent years and makes its home in a decommissioned 1936 Brooklyn. subway station. You'll learn the history behind the City's subway system, board vintage subway and elevated trains and visit a working signal tower. The newer additions especially jazz kids—buses they can board and a simulated traffic intersection with traffic lights and coordinated walk/don't walk signs, parking meters and fire hydrants. The museum has created a website that invites visitors to share transit stories (the LIRR should only be so obliging) and to view photographs and even some exhibits. This is a fun museum—if you dig trains and buses.

Parent Tip

The Heart of Brooklyn Trolley stops at many Brooklyn attractions, including the Brooklyn Children's Museum. The trolley operates on Saturday, Sunday and holidays from noon to 6pm. Also, the BCM (Brooklyn Children's Museum) Trolley Express runs every hour (between 10:15am and 4:15pm) on weekends from the Grand Army Plaza.

DUMBO

DUMBO is not a flying elephant (although really young children will prefer it were). DUMBO is the acronym for *Down Under the Manhattan Bridge Overpass*, located at the heel of the Brooklyn Bridge, just five minutes from lower Manhattan.

Subway: A, G, F.

DUMBO is home to a very cool, progressive arts community, as well as a selective collection of eateries, shops and pricey residences. The views of Manhattan from DUMBO are works of art in of themselves: the Statue of Liberty, the Brooklyn and Manhattan bridges and the Manhattan skyline. There's a park that sits pretty along the river—grab a hot cocoa from **Jacque Torres Chocolate shop** and sit at this riverfront perch to soak in the intoxicating views (*see listing below*). Retailers include ABC Home and West Elm and new ones pop up practically overnight.

Food for Thought in DUMBO

• Jacques Torre Chocolate
66 Water Street, between the Brooklyn and Manhattan bridges, Tel. 718/875-9772, www.mrchocolate.com. Open: Monday through

Saturday 9am to 7pm, Sunday 10am to 6pm. Chocolate lovers die and go to heaven every day here. You can buy chocolates to go or have a seat at one of the café tables and sip hot cocoa and munch on pain au chocolats. Bonus: Torre uses no preservatives and only natural ingredients.

• Grimaldi's Pizzeria
19 Old Fulton Street (under the Brooklyn Bridge), Tel. 718/858-4300, www.grimaldis.com. Open: Sunday through Thursday 11:30am to 10:45pm, Friday 11:30am to 11:45pm and Saturday noon to 11:45pm. Think red-checkered tablecloths and out-of-this-world thin crust pizza that's made in coal brick ovens.

A heads-up for ice cream lovers: One of my closest friends, who lived in nearby Brooklyn Heights for about ten years, insists that the best ice cream is at the **Brooklyn Ice Cream Factory** at Fulton Ferry Landing (between Old Fulton and Water streets; Tel. 718/246-3963.) There are only eight flavors to choose from, (refreshing in itself), especially for kids who are prone to meltdowns when bombarded with too many choices.

BRONX

Yes, the Bronx is up—uptown that is. And it's home to one of the city's most celebrated landmarks, Yankee Stadium, as well as the world-famous Bronx Zoo.

We're frequent visitors to the Bronx to see the Yankees play. And there's no better place in October than in the Bronx. Forget leaf peeping in New England, if the Yankees are in the playoffs and/or World Series, this is the best spot to appreciate the crisp autumn air.

The Bronx gets a bad rap (no pun intended as this is also where rap music is enjoyed on the streets and in clubs) as being a place where you shouldn't go. But if you know where to go in the Bronx, you'll discover it to be a vibrant part of the fabric of the City.

In fact, while most people envision the Bronx to be a giant maze of concrete, the Bronx actually has more parkland than in any of the other boroughs, including the incredible New York Botanical Garden—250 acres that include 27 specialty gardens and a stunning 50-acre forest. Wave Hill, a pretty public garden and cultural institution is also in the Bronx.

Of course, the Bronx Bombers who play at Yankee Stadium call this borough home. As do the 4,000 animals that live at The Bronx Zoo, the largest urban zoo in the country dating back to 1899. And many celebs have lived here including Tony Curtis, Ann Bancroft, Regis Philbin, Lou Gehrig, Edgar Allan Poe (you can visit his house), Mark Twain, John F. Kennedy and Ralph Lauren.

Settled in 1639 and named for Swedish settler, Jonas Bronck, the Bronx has about 60 historic sites and landmarks (several are listed below).

Yankee Stadium

161st Street and River Avenue, Tel. 718/293-6000, www.yankees.com.
Subway: 4, B, D to 161st street which is directly at Yankee Stadium.
Ferry: New York Waterway, 800/53-FERRY, www.nywaterway.com.

Last chance to see Yankee Stadium before it becomes the new and better Yankee Stadium beginning with the 2009 season. The House that Ruth Built is one of the city's most famous landmarks. It is also, in some ways, a shrine to the legacy of the Yanks—and the history of baseball—even for those of you who aren't Yankee fans (you know who you are) but love the game.

The Stadium opened on April 18, 1923 when the Yankees played against, who else, the Red Sox. The rest, as they say, is history. The Yankees have gone on to win 26 championships (at press time; hopefully 27 to usher out the old stadium).

Most Major League Baseball players agree that there is an unexplained mystique when playing at this ballpark. Baseball fans, too, appreciate a game played here. We've been to many ballparks, but there's something magical about watching a game at Yankee Stadium. Lots of families even plan their vacation to the City when the Yankees will be in town; check the Yankee's home game-schedule at www.yankees.com.

We're big baseball fans and especially love the Yankees. The Yankees drafted my son's father out of college. My great-grandfather and great-uncle both played in the Major Leagues for 13 years. Baseball is in our blood. Whenever we get Yankees tickets, we always arrive when the gates open, hours before the game, to take in batting practice; you might also snag player autographs if you arrive early.

Another reason to get to the stadium way before the first pitch is to rub Babe Ruth's head in **Monument Park** (Roger Clemens rubbed his head before each outing). Before each game, they line up to visit Monument Park, but the line moves quickly, so don't be put off by the crowd.

If the Yanks aren't in town or you don't want or can't go to a game, you can still take a tour to see the famous stadium. Bonus: The tours are given year-round. The **Classic Tour** includes field access, and visits to the dugout, the press box, Monument Park and the Clubhouse. Cost: Adults $20, kids (14 years old and under $15, and senior citizens (60 years old and older) $15. There are two other tours that, in addition to the above visits, include things like a movie about the Yankees history, but these tours are limited to groups. You can buy tickets online for the tour at Ticketmaster, otherwise purchase your tickets at the Stadium's Advance Ticket Windows but there is no guarantee of ticket availability. There are other restrictions, such as no tours on game days. Check the website for more specifics and updated information.

Note: Tickets to games are expensive and prohibitive for some families. Good news: There are certain games with discounted ticket prices. Check the webite for updated info. The Bleacher seats are the cheapest but there's another price to pay—the bleacher creatures: a rowdy (although good-natured) crowd. If you've got young kids and are concerned about raucous seatmates, reserve seats in the alcohol-free section. But security at the stadium is tight and the crowd generally behaves.

A great New York moment: The minute the game ends, win or lose, the classic song *New York, New York* is blasted throughout the speakers—several times while the mass exodus of baseball fans occurs. Note: Frank Sinatra's version of New York is played if the Yankees win; if they lose it's someone else (shame on me for not knowing; hopefully they'll win if you take in a game so you won't know what I'm talking about). We always stay put in our seats to soak it all in (no matter if they've won or lost) for as long as we can—eventually we're asked to leave. As you can imagine, the subway platforms are packed, so what's the rush? Savor the moment.

Hot Dog Note: You can buy hot dogs and other standard stadium fare like fries, soda, chicken sandwiches and pizza in Yankee Stadium—but it'll cost you practically as much as the ticket to get in. And, thanks to tight security, you are not allowed to bring in cans, bottles and huge picnic spreads. Still, baseball without a hot dog is practically sacrilegious. Time to compromise. There's a hot dog vendor just outside the stadium (by the giant baseball bat) who sells good dogs and the prices are lower.

Final Note: The new Yankee Stadium will open next door in time for the 2009 season.

The Bronx Zoo/Wildlife Conservation Park

Bronx River Parkway and Fordham Road, Tel. 718/367-1010, www.bronxzoo.com.

Open: Monday through Friday 10am to 5pm, Saturday and Sunday 10am to 5:30pm. November through March Monday through Friday 10am to 4:30pm, Saturday and Sunday 10am to 4:30pm and holidays 10am to 4:30pm. Open 365 days a year.

Admission: $14 adults, $10 seniors/students and kid (three years old through 12 years old), kids under three are free. Budget Tip: Wednesday is pay-what-you-wish day. Note: If you plan to visit The Congo Gorilla Forest, the cost is an extra $3.

Subway: 2, 5.

If you're zoo lovers, you'll flip for this animal kingdom. It's the largest urban zoo in the United States (265 acres) and is home to thousands of animals, birds, fish and reptiles. The Bronx Children's Zoo, a zoo within a zoo, is a big hit with kids who can pet domesticated animals and ride camels. The sea lion and penguin feedings are also big hits. The **Congo Gorilla Forest** is another popular attraction. My son loves the tram and monorail rides that crisscross the zoo.

The **Butterfly Garden** features more than 1,000 North American butterflies. Kids love to ride the grasshoppers and ladybugs at the Zucker

Bug Carousel exhibit. New exhibit: Tiger Mountain, a habitat for the zoo's Siberian tigers. Oh my!

One of the most exciting adventures in town is at the **Family Overnight Safari** here (for kids five years old and up.) You get to spend the night in a tent *outside* at the zoo. The safari is offered three times a year between the months of May through September. To register, go to www.bronxzoo.com/ bz-education; the program fills up fast so it's wise to book way ahead. Cost: $280 for adult/child pair. (Central Park Zoo offers a similar program; see separate listing).

Cloisters Museum

99 Margaret Corbin Drive, Fort Tryon Park, Tel. 212/923-3700, www.metmuseum.org. Note: see page 71 for map location.

Open: Tuesday through Sunday 9:30am to 5:15pm; November through February closing time is 4:45pm. Closed Mondays, Thanksgiving, Christmas and New Year's Day.

Admission: $20 adults, $15 seniors, and free for kids 12 years old and younger.

Subway: A to 190th Street, then M4 bus to Fort Tryon Park-The Cloisters stop.

A branch of the Metropolitan Museum of Art is one indication that this gem is classy and top notch (*see photo on next page*). The Cloisters sits pretty in a four-acre setting on a hilltop peering over the Hudson River in Fort Tryon Park. The setting is one reason to visit. There are others: It's the only museum in America devoted exclusively to medieval art. And the **Unicorn tapestries** are really cool. Technically it's located on Manhattan's northernmost tip, but I'm including it in the Bronx section, because it's a schlep from Manhattan's main tourist zones and it's practically in the Bronx.

Wave Hill

675 West 252nd Street (at Independence Avenue), Bronx, Tel. 718/549-3200, www.wavehill.org.

Open: Tuesday through Sunday 9am to 4:30pm. From mid-April to mid-October open until 5:30pm, and June through August open on Wednesday until 9pm. Closed Monday.

Admission: Free on Saturday mornings, all day Tuesday. Wednesday through Sunday and Saturday afternoons, $6 adults, $3 students and seniors, $2 kids six years old and older, free for kids ages 6 years and under.

Train: MetroNorth to Riverdale station.

A sprawling, 28-acre public garden with views of the Hudson River and the Palisades, woos families on sunny days. Let 'em loose: kids can roam the pretty gardens and lawn. Bonus: **Family Art Projects** (1pm to 4pm weekends) in horticultural and the arts for kids. Advance reservations are not required.

Edgar Allan Poe Cottage

East Kingsbridge and Grand Concourse, Bronx, Tel. 718/881-8900, www.bronxhistoricalsociety.org.

Open: Saturday 10am to 4pm and Sunday 1pm to 5pm.

Admission: $3 adult, $2 seniors and kids.

Subway: D, 4.

If your children love poetry, they'll be interested in this restored home of Edgar Allan Poe, where he wrote *Annabel Lee,* among other poems. There's a film presentation and a guided tour.

12. I'M HUNGRY!

New York City is home to some of the world's best chefs and most celebrated restaurants. After all, it is the Melting Pot of the World and as such dishes up every ethnic cuisine you can dream of. The challenge, of course, is finding a restaurant that will appeal to all family members and will not compromise your budget. The good news is there are family-friendly spots where the food, as well as the ambience, is agreeable to both parents and kids.

Budget Tip: If you're a foodie (like I am), and the key to a great vacation for your family is eating well, consider planning your visit to New York during one of the city's Restaurant Weeks—typically held in late January or early February and then again in June. The way it works: More than 200 restaurants throughout the city offer a reduced set price for lunch and dinner. The best part: The lineup includes the most sought after, priciest restaurants in town. For more info, call or visit www.nycvisit.com

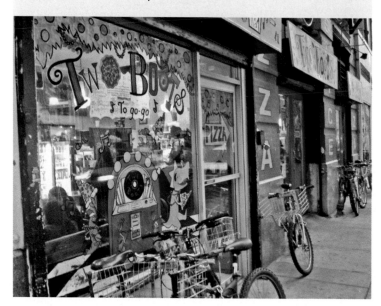

LOWER MANHATTAN

McDonald's

160 Broadway, Tel. 212/385-2063. $

Yep, it's a McDonald's, but there' a white gloved doorman and a piano player at this Mickey D's in the Financial District. Afterall, powerful stockbrokers and City Hall government officials chow down on Big Macs at this Golden Arches. Kids, of course, get a kick out of the fanciness of it all.

The Soda Shop

125 Chambers Street, Tel. 212/571-1100. $

Open: Monday through Friday 7pm to 10pm, Saturday 8am to 10pm and Sunday 8am to 8pm.

Retro ice-cream parlor that serves thick milk shakes, egg creams and lime rickeys. There's also food on the menu like pot pies and soups.

The Incredible Daisy May's BBQ!

When visiting the Big Apple the temptation is strong to stop for a quick and cheap meal at one of New York's hot dog and knish vendors. They're everywhere. But, if you're in the **midtown area,** do like the movers and shakers: head for the **Daisy May's BBQ USA** cart parked at 50th Street between Sixth and Seventh avenues for a cup of gourmet chili that'll have you swear you're in the Lone Star State. The chef, Adam Perry Lang, is a Daniel Boulud-trained chef (translation: excellent pedigree). The chili is served with homemade hot sauce and a flour tortilla, and you can order a side dish of beans. Cost: $7 for a 12-ounce cup.

Bonus: To enjoy your chili while sitting outside in a small park with a waterfall and a piece of the Berlin Wall in it (yep, the Berlin Wall), walk a couple of blocks to 53rd Street just off Fifth Avenue, on the north side across the street from the Harper Collins Building. There is also a Daisy May's BBQ restaurant at 623 11th Avenue (at 46th Street) where you can order brisket, ribs, chicken and all the fixins (Tel 212/977-1500).

LITTLE ITALY

Umberto's Clam House

178 Mulberry Street (corner of Broome Street), Tel. 212/431-7545, www.umbertosclamhouse.com. $$

Open: Daily 11am to 4pm.

Clams (baked, littleneck, cherrystones) are only half the story at this popular Italian restaurant specializing in Italian seafood specialties. Umberto's has been on the scene in Little Italy way before *The Sopranos* made it big.

Casa Bella Ristorante Bar-Cafe

127 Mulberry Street (between Hester and Canal streets), Tel. 212/431-4080, www.casabellarestaurant.com. $$

Open: Sunday through Thursday noon to midnight, Friday and Saturday noon to 1am.

Mangia here May through October and you're in for a real treat when the outdoor café is open. No matter what time of year you visit though, the food is what you'd expect from a popular Italian restaurant in Little Italy with a traditional menu: antipasto, spaghetti, manicotti, tortellini, fettuccine, ravioli with delicious sauces, as well as hearty meat and seafood dishes.

Lombardi's

32 Spring Street (between Mott and Mulberry Streets), Tel. 212/941-7994. $

Open: Sunday through Thursday 11:30am to 11pm, Friday and Saturday 11:30am to midnight.

Practically since the beginning of time, this popular

Little Italy pizza joint has been rolling out and rolling in the dough. You want a good New York pizza pie? You come here.

CHINATOWN

Chinatown is spot-on for **dim sum**, the Cantonese term for small dishes meaning "a little bit of heart." There are hundreds of types of steamed and fried dim sum (meat, vegetarian, fish). Usually you select from carts that are pushed throughout a dim sum restaurant.

Jing Fong

20 Elizabeth Street (between Canal and Bayard streets), Tel. 212/964-5256. $$

Open: Monday through Friday 10:30am to 3:30pm and 5pm to 11pm, Saturday and Sunday 9am to 3:30pm and 5pm to 11pm.

 A hugely popular Chinatown restaurant in an equally large space—eating here is an event, not just a meal. You must experience dim sum here—carts with more than 100 dim sum items are whizzed around the room by the hi-tech waitstaff who wear microphone headsets. You'll see lots of Chinese families dining at this festive restaurant.

Golden Unicorn

18 East Broadway (at Catherine Street). Tel. 212/941-0911. $$

Open: Monday through Friday 10am to 10:30pm, Saturday and Sunday 9am to 11pm, dim sum is served daily between 9am and 3:30am.

Another very popular Chinatown dim sum hot spot—the selection is enormous and so is the dining space.

Triple Eight Palace

88 East Broadway (between Division and Market streets), Tel. 212/941-8886. $$

Yep, dim sum is the name of the game at this popular restaurant, too.

Great New York Noodletown

28 1/2 Bowery (at Bayard St.), Tel. 212/349-0923. $$

Open: Monday through Sunday 9am to 4am.

You won't find dim sum here, but if your kids love noodles this is a good choice. Think noodle soup, pan fried noodles, lo mein. The restaurant is also known for its salt baked shrimp.

Chinatown Ice Cream Factory

65 Bayard Street (between Mott and Elizabeth streets), Tel. 212/608-4170.

Open: Sunday through Saturday 11am to 10pm or 11pm (depending on the weather).

Not your traditional ice cream flavors (green tea, taro and lychee), but there's vanilla, too.

SOHO / TRIBECA / THE VILLAGE

Balthazar

80 Spring Street (between Crosby and Broadway streets), Tel. 212/965-1414, www.balthazarny.com. $$$.

Open: Breakfast Monday through Friday 7:30am to 11:30pm, Saturday and Sunday 8am to 10am; lunch Monday through Friday noon to 5pm; dinner Monday through Thursday 5:45pm to 1am, Sunday 5:30pm to midnight; after hours Monday through Thursday midnight to 1am, Friday and Saturday 5:45pm to 2am.

This French bistro-style restaurant with its red leather banquettes, smoky mirrors and *joie de vivre* mood is one of my favorite places to eat in the city. And I'm not alone; this is one of the most popular restaurants in town. Come for breakfast and your kids will love the Nutella on a baguette. Your kids will also adore the *steak frites* (french fries), believed by many food critics to be the best in town. The raw bar at Balthazar is incredible; 75 types of oysters. Balthazar is open until the wee hours of the morning—fun if you've got older teens who want to go somewhere hip after a Broadway show or Yankee or Met game, for instance. Tables are close together—you may rub elbows (figuratively and literally) with New York celebs. *C'est la vie* in the Big City.

Note: You will be hugely disappointed, as we were recently, if you don't make reservations and expect to be seated during peak times (translation: most of the day).

Zoe

90 Prince Street (between Broadway and Mercer streets), Tel. 212/966-6722, www.zoerestaurant.com. $$.

Open: Lunch Monday through Friday noon to 3pm; dinner Tuesday through Thursday 6pm to 10:30pm, Friday 6pm to 11pm, Saturday 5:30pm to 11pm, Sunday 5:30pm to 10pm; brunch Saturday and Sunday 11:30am to 3pm.

We settled into a booth in this pleasant restaurant, nibbled over food we'd ordered from the American-cuisine-inspired menu, and lingered for hours. There are also tables, but there is something about a booth that's almost like a high chair—kids are a captive audience when they sit in a booth. The open kitchen with a wood burning oven, grill and rotisserie also brings everyone together—especially kids who can opt to sit at the Chef's Counter and order off the Kid's Dinner Menu, as well as have the restaurant's culinary team explain to them the cooking process. The non-traditional kids' menu includes fun, experimental things like: Zoe's famous crispy calamari and dipping sauce ($5.50), and main plates that include everything from pasta to sliced steak to free-range chicken breast. There's even a special children's house cocktail: the Pineapple Surprise.

Broome Street Bar

363 West Broadway, Tel. 212/925-2086. $

Open: Sunday through Thursday 11am to 1:30am, Friday and Saturday 11am to 2:30am, Saturday and Sunday 11am to 4pm.

A favorite haunt of locals (you almost expect Norm from *Cheers* to swing through the doors), you can't miss at this Soho institution (it's been here more than 35 years) with its comforting neighborhood ambience. When I lived down the street I'd hang here often. Think burgers ($8.75 and up), sandwiches like a tuna melt ($8.50) and creative salads ($9.75). Broome Street also serves a popular brunch on Saturday and Sunday between 11am and 4pm.

Bubby's Pie Co.

120 Hudson Street (at North Moore Street), Tel. 212/219-0666, www.bubbys.com. $ There is also a location in DUMBO.

Open: Breakfast, lunch and dinner daily.

Buttermilk pancakes, potato pancakes, meatloaf, fried chicken and incredible pies all served in a we-are-family atmosphere.

Pearl Oyster Bar

18 Cornelia Street (between Bleeker and West 9th streets), Tel. 212/691-8211, www.pearloysterbar.com. $$

Open: For lunch, Monday through Friday noon to 2:30pm; and for dinner Monday through Saturday 6pm to 11pm.

Oddly, there aren't *that* many seafood restaurants in this city, despite the fact that it's an island surrounded by water and the Atlantic Ocean is a subway ride away. Pearl Oyster Bar is one of only a handful of great seafood spots in Manhattan—lobster and oyster rolls, mussels in a mustard and wine cream sauce are specialties. It's tiny (even though it has been expanded) and you'll wait for a table (reservations are not accepted) but if it's great seafood you crave with a cool Greenwich Village vibe, it's worth your while.

John's Pizzeria

278 Bleeker Street, Tel. 212/243-1680, www. johnspizzerianyc.com. $

Open: Monday through Saturday 11:30am to 11:30pm, Sunday 11:30pm to 9pm.

I've been inhaling pepperoni slices at this way-popular pizza joint way before my son was born, and it's just as popular now as it was then. You can't order individual slices but you won't want to—it's so good you'll devour an entire pie. Order it plain or select from the more than a dozen toppings. This is the original John's Pizzeria and it's got a lived-in-look, but locals wouldn't want it any other way. A second location, at Times Square, is equally popular but glossier. The Times Square restaurant is located at 260 West 44th Street.

Peanut Butter & Co.

240 Sullivan Street, www.ilovepeanutbutter.com. $

Open: Sunday through Thursday 11am to 9pm, Friday and Saturday 11am to 10pm.

The nuttiest of sandwiches are featured on the menu here. Think: "Peanut Butter Cup," freshly ground peanut butter, kissed with a layer of Nutella. Or, "The Heat Is On Sandwich," spicy peanut butter and chilled chicken, with a bit of pineapple jam. Or, the "White Chocolate Wonderful Sandwich," white chocolate peanut butter and orange marmalade. The menu also features non-peanut butter items, including tuna fish, turkey, and grilled cheese sandwiches. The shop is on quiet Sullivan Street, an off-the-beaten-path Soho street and there are benches out front where you can munch.

Katz's Deli

205 East Houston Street (at Ludlow Street), Tel. 212/254-2246, www.katzdeli.com. $

Open: Sunday, Wednesday and Thursday 8am to 10:45pm, Monday and Tuesday 8am to 9:45pm, Friday and Saturday 8am to 2:45am.

New York's oldest deli (it dates to the late 1800's) where the pastrami and corned beef sandwiches keep 'em lined up. The hot dogs are good, too. This is a quintessential Lower East Side New York deli.

Two Boots

37 Avenue A, Tel. 212/254-1919, www.twoboots.com. $

Open: Sunday through Tuesday 11:30am to 11pm, Wednesday through Thursday 11:30am to midnight, Friday and Saturday 11:30am to 2am.

First, the name: The boots represent the geographical shapes of Italy and Louisiana. The menu: Inspired by the cuisine of both those spots.

The food is fun and spicy and the ambience is fun loving (*see photo on page 99*). Kids love the pizza—with all kinds of toppings, including the standard pepperoni to the more experimental *tasso* (Cajun ham) and BBQ shrimp. Sandwiches are also on the menu like blackened catfish Po' Boy and eggplant Parmesan.

Other Two Boots locations: Two Boots Pizzeria at 42 Avenue A; Two Boots Grand Central (in the lower level dining concourse); Two Boots to Go-Go at 74 Bleeker Street in the Village; Two Boots to Go West at 201 West 11th Street; Two Boots Rock Center at Rockefeller Center (in the lower level dining concourse). There are also several Two Boots theaters, which offer cult films in retro settings but these aren't necessarily family-friendly.

Café Milkshake

> 343 East 47th Street, www.nymilkshake.com $
> Open: Hours vary seasonally.

The delicious milkshakes and malts here are meal-worthy (yet, they also have a limited menu including grilled cheese sandwiches). Bonus: Kids love the hot waffle ice cream sandwiches.

Silver Spurs Diner

> 490 LaGuardia Place (corner of Houston), Tel. 212/228-BEEF. $
> Open: 24 hours.

Giddyap to this popular neighborhood diner and order up a stack of pancakes or a grilled cheese off the cutesy menu. The burgers are huge! Silver Spurs is the kind of place where the locals have been going forever, as well as in-the-know out-of-towners. Bonus: You can sit outside in nice weather.

Cowgirl

> 519 Hudson Street, Tel. 212/633-1133, www.cowgirlnyc.com. $$
> Open: Daily noon to midnight.

Kids love the Southwestern cuisine dished up here like corn dogs and quesadillas and the signature Frito pie (Fritos smothered in chili and cheese and served in a Frito Lay bag!). Crazy, fun, rodeo atmosphere.

'sNice

> 45 Eighth Avenue at 4th Street, Tel. 212/645-0310. $
> Open: Breakfast, lunch and dinner.

You gotta love a place where the motto is 'Be 'snice to each other.' Kiddie-sized picnic tables, Play-Doh and Yahtzee woo kids of all ages. A lot of the menu is vegan but there's also PBJ and grilled cheese and muffins and pastries. Very popular neighborhood hangout.

S'Mac

> 345 East 12th Street (between 1st and 2nd avenues), Tel. 212/358-7912, www.smacnyc.com $$
> Open: Sunday through Thurday 11am to 11pm, Friday and Saturday 11am to 1am

S'Mac (acronym for Sarita's Macaroni and Cheese) is a Godsend for parents with picky eaters. Most finicky palettes will tolerate macaroni and cheese and the All-American version will please them nicely. But macaroni and cheese is also the ultimate comfort food and many adults find pleasure in indulging every once in awhile. At S'Mac's you're treated to gourmet macaroni and cheese like goat cheese and Brie versions and you have a choice of 14 add-ins (think Kalamata olives) to suit your mac 'n cheese fantasy.

Tortilla Flats

767 Washington Street (and 12ᵗʰ Avenue), Tel. 212/243-2053, www.tortillaflatsnyc.com. $$

Open: Monday through Thursday noon to midnight, Friday and Saturday noon to 1am, Sunday noon to 11pm.

Okay, I have been coming here since I was just out of college seeking a margarita, Tex Mex and a fun place to meet friends. I was surprised to learn recently that Tortilla Flats is also a fun hotspot for families with Bingo on Monday and Tuesday nights, hula hooping on Wednesday nights and on Sunday nights it's pajama night. The kids' menu is inexpensive ($1.95 to $5.95) and features such items as a Tyranotaco (chicken and beef) and Enchiladalophysis (chicken, cheese and vegetable).

FLATIRON / UNION SQUARE / MURRAY HILL

Blue Smoke

116 East 27ᵗʰ Street (between Park Avenue South and Lexington Avenue), Tel. 212/447-7733, www.bluesmoke.com. $$

Open: Tuesday through Thursday 11:30am to 11pm, Friday and Saturday 11:30am to 1am, Sunday and Monday 11:30am to 10pm.

Ribs lovers swear by the St. Louis spareribs and Texas-style salt 'n' pepper ribs at this restaurant with its easy-going vibe.

Max Brenner: Chocolate by the Bald Man

841 Broadway (between 13ᵗʰ and 14ᵗʰ streets), Tel: 212/388-0030, www.maxbrenner.com. $$

Open: Monday through Thursday 8am to 11pm, Friday and Saturday 8am to 1am, Sunday 9am to 11pm.

In a word: chocolate. Max Brenner elevates chocolate to an art form, from the chocolate boutique in the front of the restaurant where you can buy pricey, beautiful chocolates to the restaurant's menu from which chocoholics (go ahead, admit it!) can order such goodies as a waffle dotted with berries and drizzled with caramel and hot chocolate sauce and bits of white chocolate. Don't love chocolate? No problem, do as my chocophobic son did and order the chicken sandwich. This is a fun, whimsical, touristy place that will put a smile on your face whether you have a love affair with chocolate or not. There is another location at 141 2nd Avenue (at 9th Street), which is open Monday through Thursday 10am to 11pm, Friday and Saturday 10am to 1am and Sunday 10am to 11pm.

Bonus: You can pop in just to order one of the best cups of steamy hot chocolate you've ever had and slurp it while sitting on a bar stool. My son's grandmother treated him and his cousin to lunch here—this is a perfect, feel-good inter-generation spot with great eye appeal!

Shake Shack

Madison Square Park (southeast corner at Madison Avenue and 23rd Street), 212/889-6600, www.shakeshack.com $

Open: Year-round 11:30pm to 6:30pm in the winter (later in the spring, summer and fall).

A fun-loving, outdoor restaurant with burgers, fries and yep, shakes. This is an idyllic spot for families looking for an experience that offers kid-friendly food with quintessential New York ambience—and a great view of the Flatiron Building.

2nd Avenue Deli

162 East 33rd Street (between Lexington and 3rd Avenues), Tel. 212/677-0606. $

Open: Sunday through Thursday 6am to 2am, Friday and Saturday 6am to 4am.

This famous New York landmark that dates to 1954 was closed not too long ago, much to the dismay of New Yorkers who adore the pickles and pastrami. The deli has been reborn at a new, smaller location (the old location was, yep, 2nd avenue and 10th street. Same great Kosher and New York deli specialties. Kids love the egg creams.

CHELSEA

Pastis
    9 Ninth Avenue (corner of Little West 12th Street), Tel. 212/929-4844, www.pastisny.com. $$
    Open: Breakfast 8am to 11:30am daily; lunch noon to 6pm Monday through Friday; brunch 10am to 4:30pm Saturday and Sunday; dinner 6pm to midnight daily; supper midnight to 1am Sunday through Wednesday, midnight to 2am Thursday and midnight to 3am Friday and Saturday.
    In the heart of the trendy Meatpacking District, this incredibly popular brasserie is celeb central. Owned by the same owners as Balthazar (see separate listing), Pastis is a treat—and is especially popular with Europeans living in or visiting the City. There are always kids in high chairs when we come here. Provencal cuisine is the thrust of the menu, but there are kid-friendly items. Bonus: The bathroom is cool—there are separate men's and women's toilets but you'll eventually meet at the shared trough-like sink. Guaranteed for kid giggles.

Empire Diner
    210 10th Avenue (at West 22nd Street), Tel. 212/243-2736. $$
    Open: Daily 24 hours (except on Tuesdays between 4am and 8am).
    When this diner in an old rail car first opened decades ago, it was a magnet for celebrities. Today, it still has a force, thanks to its outdoor seating and show tunes. The food isn't standard diner fare—in fact, don't come here for pancakes (they aren't on the menu, to many people's chagrin). Empire is a pretentious diner with a menu that's more akin to a nice restaurant than a New York City diner.

TIMES SQUARE / THEATER DISTRICT

ESPN Zone
    1472 Broadway, Tel. 212/921-ESPN, www.espnzone.com. $$
    Open: Sunday 11am to 11pm, Monday through Thursday 11:30am to 11pm, Friday 11:30am to midnight, Saturday 11am to midnight.
    Sports lovers will score big at this thick-in-the-action Times Square hot spot. The kid's menu offers sports-themed items such as "sliders" and two mini cheeseburgers.

Café Edison

228 West 47th Street (in the Hotel Edison), Tel. 212/840-5000, www.edisonhotelnyc.com. $

Open: Monday through Saturday 6am to 9:30pm, Sunday 6am to 7:30pm.

A venerable New York hangout, with actors, producers and magicians who gather to talk shop, swap opening night stories and dine on homemade soups (matzo ball, borscht), sandwiches and burgers. Great spot to grab a bite to eat before the theater.

Planet Hollywood Times Square Restaurant & Bar

1540 Broadway (at 45th Street), Tel. 212/333-STAR, www.planethollywood.com. $$

Open: Sunday through Thursday 11am to midnight, Friday and Saturday 11am to 1am.

Ribs, burgers, movie memorabilia and movie displays, this popular tourist spot moved from its midtown location to Times Square. Founders Demi Moore, Arnold Schwarzenegger, Sylvester Stallone and Bruce Willis expanded this concept all over the country, so chances are you're already familiar with the theme. There's a standard kid's menu of macaroni and cheese and other items that are not alien to youngsters.

Red Lobster

5 Times Square, Tel. 212/730-6706, www.redlobster.com. $$$

Open: Lunch 11am, dinner 4pm.

Chances are you're way familiar with this seafood chain—but this is the glitziest of them all. The Times Square restaurant spans three-levels and has in a short time become one of the most popular spots to dine in Times Square. Two, 420-gallon aquariums and a revolving, 10-foot tall neon-lit lobster splash things up a couple of notches. They line up to get in. I feel compelled to include this chain restaurant because it is family-friendly. However, it goes without saying, in a city like New York, with gazillion restaurants, Red Lobster probably isn't high on your list.

Ruby Foo's

1626 Broadway (at 49th Street), Tel. 212/489-5600, www.brguestrestaruants.com. $$$

Open: For lunch, daily 11:30am to 5pm; dinner Sunday through Thursday 5pm to 11; Friday and Saturday 5pm to midnight.

This three-level, upbeat pan-Asian restaurant is a crowd-pleaser with its Japanese, Chinese, Thai menu and spirited atmosphere. Thanks to its Times Square location and eye-bulging Asian-inspired décor, this eatery gets busy; reservations are recommended. Bonus: Crayons and coloring books for impatient youngsters. There is a second Ruby Foo's location uptown at 2182 Broadway (at 77th Street), Tel. 212/724-6700.

Virgil's BBQ

152 West 44th Street (between 6th and Broadway), Tel. 212/921-9494, www.virgilsbbq.com. $$

Open: Sunday through Monday 11am to 11pm, Tuesday through Friday 11:30am to midnight, Saturday 11am to midnight.

Owned by the same folks who own the incredibly successful Carmine's Italian restaurants, Virgil's steals hearts of those who have a hankering for great barbecue. The menu features hard-core, finger-lickin' barbecue like Memphis pork ribs, Owensboro lamb, Maryland smoked ham, biscuits, cornbread, grits and barbecue beans. Save room for the pecan pie. Smack those lips.

Carmine's

200 West 44th Street (between 7th and 8th avenues), Tel. 212/221-3800, www.carminesnyc.com. $$

Open: Sunday 11am to 11pm, Monday 11:30am to 11pm, Tuesday 11:30am to midnight, Wednesday 11am to midnight, Thursday and Friday 11:30am to midnight, Saturday 11am to midnight.

Southern Italian food served family-style (big platters) in a lively, festive setting. Any Italian dish you can dream up is on the menu. Promise. A feel-good, kind of place that families love. *Pass the veal parm please.* Note: There's another Carmine's on the Upper West Side at 2450 Broadway (between 90th and 91st street), Tel. 212/362-2200; open Sunday through Thursday 11:30am to 11pm and Friday and Saturday 11:30 to midnight.

Havana Central

151 West 46th Street (between Sixth and Seventh avenues), Tel. 212/398-7440. $$$

Open: Monday Tuesday and Sunday noon to 11pm, Wednesday through Saturday noon to 1am.

Cuba spices up Times Square in a big way with this spacious restaurant that serves a fabulous *ropa vieja* (stew) as well as Cuban burgers for the kids.

MIDTOWN

Casa Cupcake

545 9th Avenue (between 40th and 41st streets), Tel. 212/465-1530, www.cupcakecafe.com. $

Open: Monday through Friday 7am to 7pm, Saturday 8am to 7pm, Sunday 9am to 5pm.

The icing on the cake at this eatery in the neighborhood, once known as Hell's Kitchen, is quite literally the icing on the cake. You'll want to make the trip here just for the buttercream frosted cupcakes. Yes, you can order from a limited menu (soups and pasta), but it's the iced cupcakes that'll rope you in. Note: There is another location at 18 West 18th Street (between 5th and 6th avenues).

Jekyll and Hyde

1409 Avenue of the Americas, Tel. 212/541-9505, www.eerie.com. $$

Open: Sunday 11:30am to 11pm, Monday through Thursday 11:30am to 11pm, Friday 11:30am to 1am, Saturday 11am to 1am.

We celebrated my son's 8th birthday in this kooky restaurant and Alex loved it. It's a theme restaurant, so expect lots of Jekyll and Hyde-inspired fun. The menu's predictable though, with whimsically named items like The Mummy—"sirloin bandaged in your choice of cheese." The kid's menu (10 and younger) features pizza, chicken finger, PBJ and pasta. There are also offerings of yellow fin tuna and rib eye steak for adults. Kids adore this place, but note that it can be a scary experience for toddlers and infants. There's a Greenwich Village sidekick but it's much smaller and not nearly as good.

Ellen's Stardust Diner

1650 Broadway (at 51st Street), Tel. 212/956-5151, www.ellensstardustdiner.com. $$

Open: Monday through Thursday 7am to midnight, Friday through Saturday 7am to 1am, Sunday 7am to 11pm.

The singing waitstaff is one of the lures of this retro 1950's-themed diner (you can't miss it, its exterior is dolled up in bright red and blue). Other treats: an indoor choo-choo that snakes around the eatery's mezzanine, videos from 1950's shows, and a fun menu of typical diner stuff, including blue plate specials (turkey, chicken pot pie), hot dogs, deli sandwiches, grilled cheese. A kid's menu ($7.95) has standard stuff like burgers and chicken fingers.

BLT Burger

470 6th Avenue (between 11th and 12th streets), 212/243-8226, www.bltburger.com.

Open: Daily 11:30am to 11pm. $$

Most kids love burgers and milkshakes. And while there are many restaurants in town that feature both on the menu, BLT Burger wins the prize. BLT is one of the friendliest downtown restaurants for families with hefty burgers, frothy milkshakes, crunchy waffle fries—and great service, too. We curled into a booth one chilly weekend afternoon and settled in for a salmon burger and a classic beef burger—and of course waffle fries and milkshakes. **Bonus:** Adults can sip alcohol-spiked milkshakes.

Carnegie Deli

854 Seventh Avenue (at West 55th Street), 800/334-5606, www.carnegiedeli.com. $

Open: Daily 6:30am to 4am.

Home of the pastrami, Carnegie Deli is a celebrity—and tourist favorite. A bowl of crunchy dill pickles is as standard a tabletop item as the forks and knives. Matzoh ball soup and other Jewish mother specialties are also popular here.

Serendipity 3

225 East 60th Street (between 2nd and 3rd avenues), Tel. 212/838-3531, www.serendipity3.com. $$

Open: Sunday through Thursday 11:30am to midnight, Friday 11:30am to 1am, Saturday 11:30am to 2am.

*Frrrr*ozen hot chocolate ($6.50) is what put this restaurant on the map as a must-experience place for kids to try—especially kids of celebs who come here on a regular basis to celebrate birthdays. Sit upstairs or downstairs. There's also a menu of soups, salads, omelets, burgers, foot-long hot dogs…but it's the *frrrro*zen hot chocolate that keeps 'em coming back.

Mickey Mantle's Restaurant

42 Central Park South, Tel. 212/688-7777, www.mickeymantles.com. $$

This is my son's favorite New York City restaurant. It's got a great buzz about it even if you're not a baseball nut like he is. There's a lively bar in front, with the requisite television sets to watch live sports events—baseball in the summer, of course. You can also buy authentic autographed baseballs, bats and T-shirts, and other memorabilia (pricey, though). In the back there's a multi-level dining room, again with television sets strategically located. We always snag a booth and settle in for ribs and burgers. There's also the Spring Training Menu, a healthy, low fat, low-calories menu (grilled fish, pasta).

The Little League Menu is for kids 12 years and under and offers usual kid fare like chicken fingers, macaroni and cheese, pasta with tomato sauce, grilled cheese and burgers with waffle fries; every item is $8.95 and comes with a Mickey Mantle souvenir. Another thing this casual restaurant has going for it—its' location across the street from Central Park.

Mars 2112 Restaurant and Bar

1633 Broadway (at 51st Street), Tel. 212/582-2112, www.mars2112.com. $$

Open: Monday through Thursday noon to 9pm, Friday noon to midnight, Saturday 11:30am to midnight, Sunday 11:30am to 9pm.

A theme attraction cum restaurant with an alien spaceship

Parent Tip

I'm always searching for "adult" spots in Manhattan where it's perfectly acceptable to sip a glass of wine or a cocktail while kids can slurp Shirley Temples and Roy Rogers or other non-alcoholic drinks in a grown-up setting, aka cocktail lounge. I love the "Living Room" lounge at the W New York Hotel, on Lexington Avenue between 49th and 50th, a low-key scene—grab the coveted couch in front of the fireplace (on a winter's day). There are lots of living room-type chairs, as well as chessboards. There's also a reasonably priced snack menu—the fruit and cheese platter is really good. Another cool spot to sip and chat: at the lounge of the W Hotel in Times Square (47th and Broadway). A funky, red décor and white leather seating shouts out to teens that this is one hip place.

hanging over the entrance, kids will beg you to eat here. Be prepared for an outer body experience when you receive the bill; prices are out of this world for standard fare of burgers and chicken (not unlike the other theme restaurants in town) but Mars 2112 won't disappoint the kids. Captain Orion entertains.

The Waldorf Astoria

301 Park Ave. (between 49and 50th streets), Tel. 212/872-4818, www.waldorf.com. $$

Afternoon tea: Children's Tea, Saturday 3pm. Cost: $22 per child, ages three to 12 years old.

Come here for tea with your princess or prince. It's a treat to sip tea and munch on delicate edibles at the Warldorf's Cocktail Terrace that overlooks the famous Art Deco lobby. Scones, finger sandwiches, pastries and, of course, tea are served. Bonus: Piano music and games.

UPPER EAST SIDE / HARLEM

Tony's DiNapoli

1606 2nd Avenue and 82nd Street (between 83rd and 84th streets), Tel. 212/861-8686.www.tonysdinapoli.com. $$

You'll know you've arrived when you spy the giant red awning from halfway down the street. This Italian restaurant dishes out family-style platters (translation: giant portions that everyone shares) of lobster fra diavolo, veal fricatta, chicken scarpiello, eggplant parmigiana, sausage and peppers... Note: There's also a Tony's DiNapoli in Times Square at 43rd Street (between 6th Avenue and Broadway); you can order individual meals at this location.

Jackson Hole

1270 Madison Avenue (at 91st Avenue), Tel. 212/427-2820, www.jacksonholeburgers.com. $$

Open: Monday through Friday 6:30am to 11pm, Saturday 8am to 11pm, Sunday 8am to 10pm.

It's real simple: Kids love Jackson Hole hamburgers. All kinds of toppings dress the seven-ounce burgers: the Eastsider is smeared with bacon, cheese, ham, mushrooms, tomatoes and fried onions; the Southwest burger is blanketed with guacamole and raw onion. Have it your way—bare or top heavy. Chicken sandwiches and salads also make a respectable showing at this beefy burger restaurant, as do blue plate specials (shrimp, steak.) And the prices are respectable: Hot dogs are $2.50. The scene is casual and there's sidewalk seating in nice weather. There are so many Jackson Hole's in the City, you'd swear you were in Wyoming. Other locations include 232 East 64th Street, Tel. 212/371-7187; 1611 Second Avenue, Tel. 212/737-8788.

Lexington Candy Shop
   1226 Lexington Avenue (at 83rd Street), Tel. 212/288-0057. $$
   Don't tell the kids you're going to a candy shop. Founded in 1925 this place is *not* a candy shop but instead, a diner with the requisite long counter where tuna melts and malteds are served. A feel good spot. When in New York you must hit a diner, and this is one of the oldest and best in town.

Sylvia's
   328 Lenox Avenue, Tel. 212/996-0660, www.sylviassoulfood.com. $$
   Open: Monday through Saturday 8am to 10:30pm, Sunday 11am to 8pm.
   For excellent soul food and clap-your-hands gospel music, head way uptown to Sylvia's in Harlem. Sylvia Woods and her family opened this joint as a 35-seat restaurant in 1962, which blossomed into a popular Harlem restaurant that seats 450 people today. Praise the food: smothered chicken, grits, fried chicken, collard greens, and Sylvia's famous BBQ ribs. Yes, there are burgers and chicken for non-adventurous kid's (or adults) palettes; kids love Sylvia's macaroni and cheese. The best day to visit: Sunday, for the gospel music brunch that sets a contagious life-is-good mood.

CENTRAL PARK

Loeb's Central Park Boathouse Restaurant
   Central Park Lake (off East 72nd Street), Tel. 212/517-2233, www.centralparknyc.org. $$-$$$
   Open: Monday through Friday noon to 4pm, 5:30pm to 9:30pm for dinner; Saturday and Sunday open 9:30am to 4pm for brunch, 6pm to 9:30pm for dinner. Open for dinner April through November.
   On a pretty day, we've eaten here outside and watched the boats sail on the Lake. New American cuisine and seafood grace the menu but it's not

the food that wins a loyal clientele, it's the lake location. After or before your meal, you can rent canoes, rowboats or take a gondola ride.

Tavern on the Green
Central Park West (at 67th Street), Tel. 212/873-3200, www.tavernonthegreen.com. $$$

Open: Lunch—Monday through Friday 11:30am to 3pm and weekends from 11am. Dinner—Sunday through Thursday 5pm to 10pm; Friday and Saturday 5pm to 10:30pm; Saturday and Sunday brunch 10am to 3pm.

Crystal chandeliers and walls of mirrors tell part of the story, but you shouldn't think this New York landmark restaurant is off-limits because it's too ritzy. Built to house sheep in the 1870's, Tavern on the Green can seat 1,500 people in its six dining rooms. The restaurant is family-friendly—if you know how to do it. From May to October you can eat al fresco in the garden or, come just for cocktails in the garden bar. The garden is the restaurant's best feature—at night the lights twinkle in the trees and, no matter what kind of day you've had in the City, you'll fall in love with Manhattan in this setting.

UPPER WEST SIDE

Gray's Papaya
2090 Broadway (at 71st Street), Tel. 212/799-0243, www.grayspapaya.com. $

Open: 24/7.

Well, let's put it this way: The food's not great but you gotta visit just once to buy a not-so-great hot dog and a cold papaya juice drink (does the job on a hot summer day). I've been coming here since the days right out of college when I lived in an illegal sublet on West 72nd street. Boy, did we have fun scarfing down those dogs and papaya drinks at this open-24-hours New York institution. I wouldn't touch one of those dogs now (and you'll be skeptical, too) but your kids will love everything about this place. It's a rite of passage kind of thing.

Dallas BBQ

27 West 72nd Street (off Central Park West), Tel. 212/873-2004, www.bbqnyc.com. $$

Open: Sunday through Thursday 11am to 2am, Friday and Saturday 11am to 1am.

I've eaten many times here—before I had kids and with kids. It's one of the best values in town. Start off with a loaf of the famous onion rings (Spanish onions) and move on to the rotisserie BBQ chickens (no additives, no sauces, made every hour on the hour). We usually order a quarter-chicken meal that comes with cornbread and choice of baked or fried Idaho potatoes. The cost: $5.99. Oh, the drinks here are humongous—the strawberry daiquiris are the perfect complement to the zingy barbecued chicken.

Note: Dallas BBQ has spread its wings and opened up restaurants all over town. The locations: In Times Square at 242 West 42nd Street, 212/221-9000; Tel. 212/674-4450); in the East Village at 132 Second Avenue (at St. Mark's Place; Tel. 212/777-5574); in Chelsea at West 23rd Street (and 8th Avenue; Tel. 212/462-0001); and on the Upper East side at 1265 3rd Avenue, 212/772-9393.

Popover Café

551 Amsterdam Avenue (at 86th Street), Tel. 212/595-8555, www.popover.com. $$

Open: Monday through Friday 8am to 10pm, Saturday and Sunday 9am to 10pm.

Cuddly teddy bears and fresh-from-the-oven popovers smeared with jam turn most kids on to this Upper West Side treasure—and their parents, too. I love the popovers here. Yes, the kids can hug the teddy bears that are all over the restaurant, and they can also draw portraits of the bears (or whatever they wish) with the crayons that they're given. Popovers are actually only the sidekick to a menu of sandwiches, soups and salads, and there's also a menu for children.

Sarabeth's Kitchen

423 Amsterdam Avenue (at 80th Street), Tel. 212/496-6280, www.sarabethsbakery.com. $$

Open: Monday through Saturday 8am to 11pm, Sunday 8am to 9:30pm.

Sarabeth and her husband opened Sarabeth's with the intention of selling her award-winning preserves and marmalade. Today, Sarabeth's is one of the hottest tickets in town for brunch—when we lived down the block I'd marvel at the crowds of yuppified West Siders with their *New York Times*, lined up for hours to get a seat. They're still lining up. The rustic, sprig-of-forsythia-kind-of-country-setting is refreshing and the food is consistently good (waffles, omelets, pancakes and that marvelous jam and marmalade—*see photo on next page*).

Sarabeth's popularity has taken the city by storm with other locations: Sarabeth's (east) is located at 1295 Madison Avenue (at 92nd Street), Tel. 212/410-7335 and Sarabeth's at the Whitney Museum is located at 945 Madison Avenue (at 75th Street), Tel. 212/570-3670. Another restaurant is located at 40 Central Park South, Tel. 212/826-5959 and Sarabeth's Bakery is located in the Chelsea Market at 75 Ninth Avenue (at 15th Street); Tel. 212/989-2424.

Alice's Tea Cup

102 West 73rd Street (at Columbus Avenue), Tel. 212/799-3006, www.alicesteacup.com. $

Open: Daily 8am to 8pm.

A sweet spot for kids with a menu that wins kid's hearts like Alice's Curious French Toast and crepes. This is also a great spot to experience afternoon tea for kids. The Wee Tea (for children under 10 years old) features scones, sandwiches and mousse. Note: There is another location on the East Side,

Café con Leche

726 Amsterdam Avenue (between 95th and 96th streets), Tel. 212/678-7000, www.cafeconlechenyc.com. $

Open: Daily 11am to 11pm.

Come for an authentic taste of Cuban and Dominican cuisine. Think *huevos rancheros,* Dominican fried chicken, paella, beef empanadas, *ropa vieja* (shredded beef) and *arroz con pollo* (chicken with rice.) Don't worry, if your kids are traditionalists, there are pancakes and French toast on the brunch menu. There's a second location at 424 Amsterdam Avenue (at West 80th street).

H&H Bagels

2239 Broadway (at 80th Street, this is the original location, Tel. 212/595-8003). There is another H&H at 639 West 46th Street, www.handhbagel.com. $

Open: All locations are open 24 hours a day, seven days a week.

In a word: bagel. They crank them out at H&H and smother them with cream cheeses, cold cuts, Nova lox, the works. New Yorkers will line up for H & H bagels—and your family should join them. It's bad *juju* to visit New York without eating a bagel at least once during your stay. With kids, you'll be tempted to feed them bagels breakfast, lunch and dinner. They're easy, they're cheap and they can be filled with anything from cream cheese to turkey to chopped chicken liver. Bagels fly out of the bins here so there's a good chance your bagel will be hot from the oven.

Rosa Mexicano

61 Columbus Avenue (at 62nd Street), Tel. 212/977-7700, www.rosamexicano.com. $$

Open: Monday for lunch noon to 3pm, dinner 5pm to 10pm; Tuesday through Saturday open for lunch noon to 3pm, dinner 5pm to 11:30pm.

Across the street from Lincoln Center, this huge Mexican restaurant has incredibly fresh guacamole and a fun, festive atmosphere. I dream about the guacamole at Rosa Mexicano. On the east side is the original, much smaller Rosa Mexicano; 1063 First Avenue (at 58th Street), Tel. 212/753-7407 (closed for lunch, open for dinner 5pm to 11:30pm daily) and there is a newer location at Union Square.

Columbus Bakery

474 Columbus Avenue, Tel. 212/724-6880, www.arkrestaurants.com. $

Open: breakfast, lunch and dinner.

A great spot for families to grab a table and sticky buns, bagels, croissants, omelets, oatmeal and granola and to enjoy while admiring passersby that stroll Columbus Avenue.

13. WHICH ONE IS MY ROOM?

The New York City hotel industry continues to boom as part of a significant post-9/11 rally. Fueled by a record number of visitors to Manhattan, the City has added 5,000 additional hotel rooms recently to bring its current inventory to more than 72,000.

Families will happily find a selection of hotels in all price ranges, some with kid-friendly amenities and packages. New hotels in previously untouched neighborhoods will—or recently have—debuted.

Unlike many destinations, New York doesn't really experience a true off-season or peak season. Christmas time is busy and hotel rates reflect that, but generally speaking, tourism is a year-round affair in the Big Apple and hotel rates don't fluctuate all that much. During the week, New York hotels cater to business travelers—and the higher weekday rates are indicative of that. Weekend rates are usually lower; keep this in mind when booking. Also, always request a family rate or package. You can do so by calling the hotel's reservation desk directly.

Suggestions & Price Guidelines

The difference between a view of a parking lot and a view of the Empire State building is as significant as night and day. If you can afford it, splurge for a room with a view (yes, these rooms will cost more). A travel agent can tell you which of the hotel's rooms have views and which do not. Still, if you're stuck with the view of the dumpster in the hotel parking lot, it's not the end of the world. In New York, you won't spend much time in your room anyway.

Pet-Friendly NYC!

One of the newest trends I see in the hotels in New York is how welcoming they've become to pets. Many not only accept pets, but offer doggie beds, pet menus, dog DVD's (for company when you are out of the room), even dog birthday cakes. And the city has many dog runs that your four-legged friends will love.

Parking at hotel garages is exorbitantly high. Ouch! But many hotels throw in complimentary parking with weekend packages or other special promotions.

Keep in mind, a travel agent is your best bet because they are usually keyed into the most up-to-date rates and packages.

We've arranged the hotels by price categories and are based on per night, double occupancies. Keep in mind though, that all of these hotels offer packages—seasonal, family, weekend, or theme—and the rates vary considerably for each. Be sure to inquire about packages when making reservations.

Here are my price guidelines:
- **Very Expensive**: Over $500 ****
- **Expensive**: $300 to $500 ***
- **Moderate**: $200 to $300 **
- **Inexpensive**: Under $200 *

LOWER MANHATTAN

VERY EXPENSIVE ****
Ritz-Carlton New York, Battery Park

2 West Street, Tel. 800/241-3333 or 212/344-0800, www.ritzcarlton.com, 298 room and suites. Concierge. Health club and spa. Restaurant: Yes.

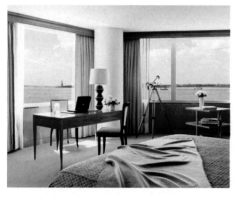

A 38-story waterfront hotel that is everything you'd expect from a Ritz-Carlton property—including the high-ticket price. The hotel has a great location—the ferries to Ellis Island and the Statue of Liberty are across the street and the New Skyscraper Museum is located in the same building as the hotel.

The Ritz Kid's program puts on the Ritz, with a teddy-bear-tuck-in at turndown (say that ten times fast), an FAO Schwartz toy menu with games, G-rated movies and entertainment and, get this, telescopes in the harborfront rooms for kids to spy on the lady across the way (The Statue of Liberty). Kids can order off a kids' menu at the restaurant.

EXPENSIVE ***

Blue Moon Hotel

100 Orchard Street, Tel. 212/533-9080, www.bluemoonyc.com. 22 rooms and suites.

This is Manhattan's only kosher hotel. Blue Moon makes its home in a meticulously restored tenement building to recreate the charm of the late 19th century Orchard Street complemented with modern amenities. Bonus: Near the highly recommended Lower East Side Tenement Museum on Orchard Street.

Millennium Hilton

55 Church Street, Tel. 800/445-8667 or 212/693-2001, www.hilton.com. 569 rooms. Restaurant: Yes. Concierge.

In the heart of the Financial District, this upscale property lived through 9/11 without any structural damage, and was restored and refurbished shortly after. It woos kids with its indoor heated lap swimming pool in a new fitness center.

New York Marriott Downtown

85 West Street, Tel. 800/242-8685 or 212/385-4900. www.marriottnyc.com. 500 rooms. Health club. Concierge. Restaurant: Yes.

Bingo: A swimming pool. A view of the Statue of Liberty is another draw, as well as affordable packages.

MODERATE **

Best Western Seaport Inn

33 Peck Slip, Tel. 800/Hotel-NY or 212/766-6600. www.seaportinn.com, 72 rooms. Fitness room. Restaurant: No.

This is a pretty hotel with a super downtown location. Complimentary continental breakfast is served each morning and coffee, tea and cookies each afternoon. Bonus: All rooms have refrigerators. Some of the rooms have terraces (not a good idea though with young kids) with views of the Brooklyn Bridge. Rooms are also equipped with Nintendo games.

Exchange Hotel

129 Front Street, 212/742-0003, www.exchangehotel.com. Restaurant: No.

A lovely boutique hotel that has a wonderful location one block from Wall Street and a two-block walk to South Street Seaport. The standard rooms are adequately sized and continental breakfast is served in the lounge.

Embassy Suites Hotel–New York City

102 North End Avenue, Tel. 800/EMBASSY or 212/945-0100, www.embassysuites.com. 463 suites. Restaurant: Yes. Fitness Center. Cinema.

Location, location, location. Located directly across the street from the World Trade Center, this hotel was forced to shut its doors following 9/11, reopening eight months later. The hotel is one of the best values for families in Manhattan with cool family packages like the Manhattan Family Museum package. In addition to being an all-suite property so families can spread out, it's located adjacent to the Battery Park Esplanade, and is in walking distance of boarding areas for the Statue of Liberty and Ellis Island ferry.

This hotel is also the official hotel of the Tribeca Film Festival and features an ambitious art collection. The in-suite amenities go the extra mile: think Starbucks Coffee. Bonus: Complimentary full cooked-to-order breakfast served each morning in Brokers Loft and a nightly Manager's Reception with complimentary beverages. The hotel complex also features family-friendly restaurants: Chevy's (a fun Mexican concept), Lili's Noodles Shop (Chinese), Pac-Rim (Japanese) and Applebees.

Tip: Request a suite with waterviews of the Hudson River and the New York Harbor.

INEXPENSIVE *
Hampton Inn Manhattan/Seaport—Financial District
320 Pearl Street, 800/HAMPTON
An intimate 65-room property located near South Street Seaport.

SOHO / TRIBECA / MEATPACKING DISTRICT

VERY EXPENSIVE ****
Hotel Gansevoort
18 Ninth Avenue (at 13th Street; considered the Meatpacking District, Tel. 877/426-7386, www.hotelgansevoort.com. 207 rooms and suites. Restaurant: Yes. Concierge. Spa and fitness center.
See photo on page 122.
If your kids must have a pool, this pricey hotel has a 45-foot heated rooftop pool with piped-in underwater music. Bliss. Another nice thing going for this property is a roof garden andpretty city and river views. The décor is modern with a twist—eel skin columns, mohair panels and leather and velvet accents set the scene. Bonus: The hotel is pet-friendly and Hudson River Park playground is a dog bone's throw away. The guestrooms feel roomy, thanks to nine-foot ceilings; feather beds are in each room. The restaurant is Japanese, which can be somewhat limiting if you don't love Japanese food. However, the hotel is a step away from Pastis and other fun, lively restaurants in the Meatpacking District.

EXPENSIVE ***
Tribeca Grand Hotel
2 Avenue of the Americas, 877/519-6600, www.tribecagrand.com. 203 rooms. Fitness center. Concierge. Restaurant: Yes.
Popular with trendsetters, the Tribeca Grand has a great location for families: walk just four blocks west and you'll hit the five-mile Hudson Park, a 550-acre park which runs along the Hudson River from Battery Park in lower Manhattan to 59th Street. The rooms aren't grand but the hotel's Sunday brunch is: Served in the Church Lounge, buffet-style, the spread features everything from shrimp to sushi to Belgian waffles. There's also a 30-seat outdoor café. The best part, though, for families: free kids' flicks shown throughout the day in the Grand Screening Room. There's also a coffee/tea/cocoa bar on each floor, as well as a video/compact disc library—and pets are welcome. Nice touch: Complimentary bicycles in the summer.

Soho Grand Hotel

310 West Broadway, 800/965-3000, www.sohogrand.com. 363 rooms. Restaurant: Yes.

A 17-story high hotel that the fashion and entertainment industries love. The hotel is also a favorite watering hole of dogs—thanks to the stone dog fountain outside the hotel's entrance. And, in addition to amenities for guests, there are pet amenities. Oh, did we mention that the Soho Grand is partly owned by Hartz Mountain Industries (as is its sister property, the Tribeca Grand)? A gourmet menu is served in what the hotel calls "Soho's Living Room," also known as the Grand Bar and Lounge; it is a place to see and be seen. Bonus: Pet goldfish upon request.

MODERATE **
Washington Square Hotel

103 Waverly Place, Tel. 800/222-0418, 212/777-9515, www.washingtonsquarehotel.com. 160 rooms. Exercise room. Concierge. Restaurant: Yes.

My mother's friends from Boston always stay at this "find" while visiting New York. The hotel is reminiscent of something you'd find in Europe: not much in the way of frills, yet clean and comfortable. Complimentary breakfast is served each morning in the bistro-like restaurant, which is a much sought after spot for dinner by locals and tourists. Bonus: Washington Square Park sits directly across the street.

CHELSEA

EXPENSIVE ***
Maritime Hotel

363 West 16th Street, Tel. 212/ 242-4300, www.themaritimehotel.com, 124 rooms and suites. Fitness center. Restaurant: Yes.

Your first clue that this is the Maritime Hotel is the porthole windows. If you'll be traveling as a single parent with one child this property will work; otherwise the standard rooms are too small for a cot and you'll need to swing for a suite. The outdoor café is a hot spot for visitors and locals on a nice day. If you and your kids like Japanese food, the wonderful restaurant Matsuri is attached. Bonus: Bicycle rentals.

INEXPENSIVE *
Hampton Inn Manhattan/Chelsea

108 West 24th Street, Tel. 800/HAMPTON or 212/414-1000, www.hamptoninn.com. 144 rooms. Fitness room. Restaurant: No.

This 20-story high rise is no-frills, with the exception of the "On the House" complimentary hot breakfast deal and "On the Run" breakfast bags. There's also free coffee and tea in the lobby 24 hours a day.

TIMES SQUARE / THEATER DISTRICT

EXPENSIVE ***
New York Marriott Marquis

1535 Broadway, Tel. 212/398-1900, www.nymarriottmarquis.com. 1,946 rooms. Fitness Center. Restaurant: Yes

The Marriott Marquis is practically a city within a city with seven restaurants and a tour/transportation desk. The hotel is centrally located in the thick of all the Times Square action. Bonus: It's got New York's only revolving lounge and restaurant. Kids love the fact that if you get up to go to the bathroom your table will be in a different spot when you return. Even if you opt not to stay here, take the kids to visit the revolving lounge for a couple of Shirley Temples and Roy Rogers; brunch and dinner are also served.

Crowne Plaza Times Square Manhattan

1605 Broadway, Tel. 800/243-6969 or 212/977-4000, www.manhattan.crowneplaza.com. 770 rooms and suites. Fitness center. Restaurant: Yes.

Ker-*ching*: A swimming pool is one of the lures for families. In-room video games is another. A busy spot with lots going on in the thick of it all.

The Paramount

235 West 46th Street, Tel. 212/764-5500, www.paramountnyc.com. Restaurant: Yes. Fitness Center.

A modern hotel with a great Times Square location. The Paramount was to recently become the Hard Rock Hotel but the transformation never happened. Cribs are available.

The Westin New York at Times Square

270 West 43rd Street (8th Avenue), Tel. 866/837-4183 or 212/201-2700, www.westinny.com. 863 rooms Fitness center and spa. Restaurant: Yes. Weekend and seasonal packages.

Steps from The Lion King, Toys 'R Us, the Yankee Clubhouse and one of the largest Mickey D's (McDonald's) anywhere, this hotel is kids' headquarters. The 45-story hotel's façade with streaks of purple and blue is pleasing to kids. The youngest children are greeted with a Westin Kids Club amenity. Teen girls will *ooh* and *ahh* over the Teen/Tween Spa Menu at the spa, with treatments like the Velvet Glow Facial and the Skin Dew body treatment. Bonus: The chain's Heavenly Beds and Heavenly Bath products are in all guestrooms.

W New York Times Square

1567 Broadway (at 47th Street), Tel. 212/930-7400, www.starwood.com. 511 rooms. Concierge. Health club.

If there aren't many of you traveling (translation: one or two parents, one child), this is a fun hotel for kids and adults. But rooms are teeny weenie. A nice touch: The Whatever/Whenever policy—if you need something (within reason), just push the Whatever/Whenever button on the phone.

The décor is very trendy and so is the clientele. Note: There are five W Hotels in the City. I personally love the W Hotels but if you've got a brood, stay elsewhere (unless you can swing for a suite or two guestrooms). Bonus: Pets are welcome and you can even order up a birthday cake for your four-legged friend.

**MODERATE **

Doubletree Guest Suites Times Square New York City

1568 Broadway, Tel. 800/325-9033 or 212/719-1600, www.doubletree.com. 460 suites. Restaurant: Yes. Fitness room. Concierge.

In a word: Suite. In a city where space is a rarity, a hotel that offers all suites for the cost of a standard room elsewhere is appreciated. Separate

Parent Tip

It's no secret, of course, that New York City is pricey. Not only are the hotels and restaurants expensive but the little things like a cup of coffee, a soda or lemonade and snacks that growing kids always seem to shout for all add up and take a big bite out of the family vacation budget. Suggestion: If the hotel you are interested in staying has a club floor, consider going for it. It'll cost more than a guestroom on a "regular" floor, but you get more than what you pay for. For example, the Crowne Plaza Times Square Manhattan hotel's Crowne Plaza Club Floor offers guests complimentary breakfast, afternoon snacks, evening hors 'd oeuvres, non-alcoholic beverages (cappuccino, espresso, sodas and juices available all day), and newspapers. Plus, there's a lounge that you can consider your living room when thing seem tight in the guestroom. Think about it: If you take advantage of the offerings, you can save a pretty bundle. Plus, on most hotel club floors, you'll get personalized attention and niceties from the club floor concierge. These special floor levels are especially popular with business travelers—and can be a great bonus for families—and many hotels offer them.

living rooms (with pullout sofa beds), dining/work areas and bedroom, refrigerator, microwave, coffeemaker, 2 TV's...home away from home. A kid's menu and a vacation station round out the family-friendly theme. Girls love the American Girl Place package.

Courtyard by Marriott–Manhattan/Times Square South
114 West 40th Street, Tel. 800/228-9290 or Tel. 212/391-0088, www.courtyardtimessquare.com. 244 rooms. Fitness center. Exercise room. Pets allowed. Concierge. Restaurant: Yes.

A pet-friendly and kid-friendly 32-story property with a complimentary breakfast buffet in the courtyard café. Complimentary coffee is served in the lobby 24/7.

Millennium Broadway Hotel New York
145 West 44th Street, Tel. 800/622-5569 or 212/768-4400, www.millenniumhotels.com. 750 rooms. Concierge. Restaurant: Yes.

Your dog or cat can stay at this very large hotel with tons of activity in the thick of the action.

Hotel 41
206 West 41st Street, Tel. 212/703-8600 or 877-847-4444, www.hotel41.com. 47 rooms. Restaurant: Yes.

Located next door to the Nederlander Theater, home to the long-running musical Rent, Hotel 41 is a boutique property with some nice touches. Complimentary espresso and cappuccino are offered daily between 4 and 7pm, and complimentary breakfast is available daily between 7am and 11am. Bonus: Pet friendly. A CD/DVD lending library is also on premises. Guestroom amenities feature Belgian bed linens and bottled spring water.

MIDTOWN

VERY EXPENSIVE ****
The Four Seasons Hotel New York

57 East 57th Street (at Park and Madison Avenues), Tel. 212/758-5700, www.fourseasons.com/newyorkfs, 368 rooms and suites. Restaurant: Yes. Spa.

Designed by I.M. Pei, this stark yet striking hotel—always a chic place for business travelers—has recently begun to woo family travelers in a big way. Kid-friendly amenities are offered to kids ages four to 17 years old. Before you arrive, provide the hotel with your child's name and the red carpet will be rolled out for them with child-sized robes and welcome amenities. Baby toiletries are also available and kids menus are offered in the restaurant and through room service.

Bonus: The concierge desk stocks a complimentary video library with children and teen videos and each guestroom has a Sony Play Station.

EXPENSIVE ***
Le Parker Meridien New York

118 West 57th Street, Tel. 800/543-4300 or 212/245-5000, www.parkermeridien.com. 730 rooms and suites. Restaurant: Yes.

Get this: Before arrival, kids can check-in with a virtual New York smart aleck concierge at http://parkermeridien.com/aleck.htm. After reservations are made, kids visit the website to find out what's happening when they'll be in town and to fill in info about what makes them tick.

Even the elevators at this hotel speak to kids; cartoons and comedy shows entertain them on the ride up and down.

Hate to leave Iggy the Lizard behind? The hotel welcomes pets of all sizes. Really. And they've even got a special pet room service menu with things like birdseed.

Shoot hoops at the hotel's gravity fitness and spa, or make a splash in the penthouse pool overlooking Central Park. Every part of this hotel

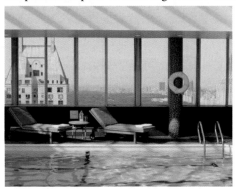

speaks to kids and adults. The hotel's restaurant, Norma's, features breakfast all day. Think: Super Cheesy French Toast and Waz-Za waffles for breakfast. Or, for total anonymity, check out the no name, no sign burger joint where burgers, fries and shakes are chowed and slurped. Visit here on Sunday and kids are in for a real treat at Seppi's Sunday choco-mania chocolate brunch.

Guestrooms are done up in slick cherry and cedar woods and have CD/DVD players.

The Alex Hotel

205 East 45th Street, Tel. 212/867-5100, www.thealexhotel.com. 203 rooms. Concierge. Fitness room. Restaurant: Yes.

This chic hotel makes a statement with limestone baths, Frederic Fekkai bath amenities and a Japanese restaurant.

Guestrooms are feng shui inspired in décor and design.

Algonquin Hotel

59 West 44th Street, Tel. 888/304-2047 or 212/840-6800, www.algonquinhotel.com. 174 rooms and suites. Concierge. Fitness center. Restaurant: Yes.

An historic hotel, you can practically taste the tradition. The Round Table Room, where literary types would spend legendary liquid lunches discussing who knows what, is still here with its cushy velvet chairs. Antique furniture and writing desks punctuate the lobby and the original marble stairs have been restored. Guestrooms are small but not cookie cutter. Family packages with combined area attractions are available.

Avalon

16 East 32nd Street, Tel. 888/HI-AVALON or 212/299-7000, www.theavalonny.com. 100 rooms and suites. Restaurant: Yes.

Not located in the most popular of neighborhoods, yet not far from Macy's and the Empire State Building, the Avalon is a tony address. A library/club room, imported Italian marble bathrooms and a discounted pass to nearby Boom Gym are some of its best features. Complimentary breakfast is included in the rate. The main reason to book this hotel: 80 of the 100 guestrooms are suites.

The Benjamin

125 East 50th Street, Tel. 212/715-2500, www.thebenjamin.com. Fitness Center and Spa, Concierge. Restaurant: Yes.

We stayed here the night before my son performed a piano recital at Carnegie Hall and had a great night's sleep (rooms are soundproof) and an enjoyable stay. All rooms are suites—a boon for families. Some nice touches: A sleep concierge with a pillow menu (you choose the type of pillow you want), and a Hasbro game cart and video library. Cute: Dogs are loved here—The Dream Dog program includes a doggie bed, doggie bathroom, even a pet psychic and Doggie DVD (which features a dog on TV that your pooch can watch while you're away from the room). Bonus: The Benjamin is part of the Affinia collection of hotels (see sidebar on page 137).

The New York Hilton Hotel

1335 Avenue of the Americas (at West 53rd Street), Tel. 212/586-7000, 800/HILTONS. Restaurant: Yes.

A huge midtown hotel that is pet friendly and family friendly with kids menus, cribs and a Vacation Station for children. Good central location.

The Michelangelo Hotel

152 West 51st Street, Tel. 212/765-0505, 800/237-0990, www.michelangelohotel.com. Restaurant: Yes. 187 rooms and suites.

An upscale, Italian-themed hotel featuring warm hospitality and family packages.

The Rockefeller Center Hotel
   25 West 51st Street, Tel. 212/262-1600. 80 rooms. Fitness center.
Restaurant: Yes. Concierge: Yes.
   This is the Rockefeller Center's first hotel and is located at the top of
Rockefeller Plaza. Many of the guestrooms have views of the ice skating
rink, Radio City Music Hall and St. Patrick's Cathedral.

MODERATE **
The Fitzpatrick Grand Central Hotel
   141 East 44th Street (at Lexington Avenue), Tel. 800/367-7701,
www.fitzpatrickhotels.com, 155 rooms and suites. Restaurant: Yes.
   If your last name begins with an "O," or you're fond of Ireland, this
hotel is your lucky four-leaf clover. Owned by an Irish company, the
Fitzpatrick Grand Central is the sister property to The Fitzpatrick Manhattan (see separate listing). This hotel serves Irish breakfast all day long in its
Irish pub, the Wheeltapper, as well as pub grub. Bonus: The hotel is a located
step from Grand Central Station. Guestrooms feature pretty canopied beds.
Bonus: The hotel offers an American Girl Experience package.

Fitzpatrick Manhattan
   687 Lexington Avenue, Tel. 800/367-7701 or 212/355-0100,
www.fitzpatrickhotels.com. 92 rooms and suites. Health club access.
Restaurant: Yes.
   The first of the NYC Fitzpatrick hotels (there are two, the other is The
Fitzpatrick Grand Central Hotel), this property's got some nice touches,
including turndown service with Irish mineral water and chocolates.
Bonus: Irish breakfast is served all day long (7am to 10:30pm daily) in the
hotel's Fitzer's restaurant. And, guests can take advantage of complimentary access to a local health and fitness club. For kids: Pay-per-view movies
and Nintendo, as well as VCR's upon request.

Jolly Hotel Madison Towers NY
   38th and Madison Avenue, Tel. 212/802-0600, www.jollymadison.com.
244 rooms, including junior suites. Spa. Concierge. Restaurant: Yes.
   Expect to be greeted with *bongiorno* or *ciao bella* instead of good
morning at this Italian-flavored boutique hotel that features all things
Italian, including an Italian-speaking staff, newspapers, an Italian breakfast
cafe with pretty red tulip chairs and granite tables and an Italian restaurant.
For kids, guestrooms feature Nintendo.

Novotel New York

226 West 52nd Street (at Broadway), Tel. 212/315-0100, www.novotel.com 480 rooms. Fitness room. Restaurant: Yes.

Novotel has a Nintendo PlayStation area for kids. For adults, one of the cool things about this hotel is that you can sit at one of the tiered terraces at the hotel's 7th floor Broadway Bar and Lounge to enjoy al fresco dining and views of Times Square (kids will also enjoy the scene).

The hotel is centrally located and within walking distance of Lincoln Center, Radio City Music Hall, Carnegie Hall and Central Park.

Radisson Lexington NY

511 Lexington Avenue at 48th Street, Tel. 800/448-4471, www.lexingtonhotelnyc.com, 705 rooms and suites. Fitness center. Concierge. Restaurant: Yes.

This modern property housed in a 1920's shell speaks to families with a collection of suites—with tons of room—and large-enough-for-a-family-of-four deluxe guestrooms.

The Blakely New York

136 West 55th Street, Tel. 212/245-1800, www.blakelynewyork.com.

A 117-room property with adequately sized rooms that have nice touches like Frette bathrobes and rainshower heads in the bathroom. There's an Italian restaurant on-site.

Parent Tip

For families on a shoestring budget, there is a collection of hotels, all in midtown, under the brand name of Apple Core. They include: La Quinta Inn Manhattan, 17 West 32nd Street; Red Roof Inn, 6 West 32nd Street; Comfort Inn Midtown, 129 West 46th Street; Super 8 Hotel Times Square, 59 West 46th Street; and the Ramada Inn East Side, 161 Lexington Avenue. Rates at these properties start at $109 per night, including continental breakfast. Kids under age 13 stay free. Make no mistake about it, these are budget properties but they do offer in-room video games, coffee makers and space—all five hotels accommodate up to four people in a room and the Super 8 Hotel Times Square features family suites. Bonus: The properties are located within walking distance of the Empire State Building, Times Square and other midtown points of interest. For more information or reservations for any of the Apple Core properties, call 800/567-7720, 212/790-2710 or visit www.applecorehotels.com.

Metropolitan Hotel NYC

569 Lexington Avenue, Tel. 212/752-7000, www.metropolitanhotelnyc.com. 755 rooms.

This property was repositioned as a Doubletree Hotel following a $30 million renovation. Kids are welcomed with cookies and check-in.

INEXPENSIVE *

Hampton Inn Manhattan/Madison Square Garden Area

116 West 31 Street at Sixth Avenue, Tel. 800/HAMPTON, www.hamptoninn.com.

A 136-room-property near Macy's and Penn Station. Translation: Very busy area.

UPPER EAST SIDE

VERY EXPENSIVE ****

The Taj Pierre New York

Fifth Avenue (at 61t street), Tel. 212/940-8111, www.tajhotels.com. Fitness center. Concierge. Fitness center. Restaurant: Yes.

A stunning property that overlooks Central Park, The Pierre offers kids a welcome amenity, milk and cookies, child-size robes, baby/kids bath toiletries and kids menus.

The Carlyle

35 East 76th Street, Tel. 800/ROSEWOOD or 212/744-1600, www.thecarlyle.com. 179 rooms and suites. Restaurant: Yes. Fitness center, concierge.

A Grande Dame-type hotel, this is one of New York's most elegant hideaways with rich carpets, chintz drapery and traditional décor. Try and

get a room that overlooks nearby Central Park—a big draw in staying here. Bonus: Kids love Madeline's Tea Party held Wednesday through Sunday 1pm to4pm. Sweet: If your name is Madeline, the tea party is free for you.

The Regency

540 Park Avenue at 61st Street, Tel. 212/759-4100, www.loewshotels.com 351 rooms and 85 suites. Fitness center. Restaurant: Yes.

A Park Avenue hotel that loves kids. The hotel features Fisher Price toys and also talks to the fussiest of travelers—teenagers. Teens receive a complimentary "T. Loews" amenity kit that includes a Loews logo bag and drink bottle, among other things.

MODERATE **

Hotel Wales

1295 Madison Avenue, Tel. 866-WALES-HOTEL or 212/876-6000, www.waleshotel.com. Fitness studio.

This century-old hotel is located a stroll's distance away from Central Park and the Metropolitan Museum of Art and the Guggenheim Museum. Nice touches: a signature drink upon arrival, complimentary espresso/cappuccino 24-hours day, complimentary bottle of water, complimentary video/CD library (each room has a VCR), complimentary continental breakfast, fitness studio and access to the 92nd Street Y ($15 a day). Bonus: Sarabeth's, one of the most popular brunch spots for Upper East Siders, is located in this hotel. Now, the bad news: the rooms are tiny, so you may have to book a suite.

Parent Tip

There is a cool collection of hotels in the City under the umbrella company, Affinia (www.affinia.com). These properties are all suite hotels and a great value for families—they range from very pricey to moderately priced. They include:

- Affinia Dumont
150 East 34th Street, Tel. 212/481-7600
- The Benjamin
(see separate write-up)
- Eastgate Tower
222 East 39th Street, Tel. 212/687-8000
- Affinia Gardens
215 East 64th Street, Tel. 212/355-1230
- Affinia 50
155 East 50th Street, Tel. 212/751-5710
- Shelburne Murray Hill
303 Lexington Avenue, Tel. 212/689-5200
- Affinia Manhattan
371 Seventh Avenue, Tel. 212/563-1800
- Surrey Hotel
(see separate listing)

Surrey Hotel
20 East 76th Street, Tel. 212/288-3700, www.affinia.com. 131 rooms and suites. Concierge. Fitness center. Restaurant: Yes.

Every single room or suite at this nothing-fancy-hotel-with-a-fancy-Upper-East-Side-address has a kitchenette or kitchen with a fridge—which can translate to huge savings for a family. One of Manhattan's best restaurants is located downstairs in the Surrey: Café Boulud (pricey but extraordinary). Check out the family package.

UPPER WEST SIDE

VERY EXPENSIVE **
Mandarin Oriental New York
80 Columbus Circle, Tel. 212/805-8800, www.mandarinoriental.com. 251 rooms and suites. Spa. Restaurant: Yes.

For some vacationing families, a hotel without a pool is like a vacation without a vacation. This elegant property has a 75-foot naturally lighted

indoor lap pool—but it'll cost you, as this is one of the most expensive hotels in the city. It makes it home at the top of the swanky Time Warner Center, affording guests with stunning views of Central Park, the City and the Hudson River. Check out the Mini-Manhattan Family Package. Amenities include baby toiletries, child-size robes and video games. If you can splurge, get a load of the bathroom in the presidential suite (*see photo on next page*)!

EXPENSIVE *
Courtyard by Marriott Upper East Side
410 East 92nd Street at York Avenue, Tel. 212/410-6777, www.marriott.com. 226 rooms and suites. Fitness center with pool. Restaurant Yes.

Location is everything with this hotel, a hop, skip and jump from Museum Mile. A 50-foot indoor lap pool is a bonus.

MODERATE**

The Milburn Hotel

242 West 76th Street (between West End Avenue and Broadway), Tel. 212/362-1006, 800/833-9622

A family-friendly hotel thanks to all suites with kitchenettes (save money on eating out) and complimentary use of an indoor swimming pool located one block away. Amenities include PlayStation2, a library with children's books and complimentary continental breakfast.

14. FIELD TRIPS

I've prepared a number of excursions for you that are outside of the City. If you want the beach, there's Jones Beach *(see photo below)* and the Hamptons on Long Island. If you want to see an old seaport village, head to Mystic Seaport in Connecticut. In Westchester, you can visit magnificent estates and homes in the Hudson Valley and in New Jersey you can take the kids to the Liberty Science Center and Six Flags. Travel farther to upstate New York to discover Cooperstown, home to the one and only Baseball Hall of Fame, as well as a lineup of other attractions to cheer about.

LONG ISLAND

In a word: Beach. Because Long Island is surrounded by water—the Long Island Sound on the North Shore and the Atlantic Ocean on the South—there are more-than-you-can-count sunny strands here for city slickers to worship the sun.

Celebrities and jaded New Yorkers who escape the steamy city heat and the frenetic city beat, travel east from New York City to **the Hamptons**, a sandy playground for the stars. The Hamptons (also known as the Island's South Fork) are also perfect antidotes to the hectic touring pace of the City for tourists—if you have the luxury of time to enjoy both city and sea.

Long Island's **North Fork** has also become a popular getaway in recent years, thanks to its many wineries and sweet villages with hotels, restaurants and farmstands. While the Hamptons are the place to see and be seen for Type A personalities, the scene on the North Fork is for low profile, low-maintenance sorts.

There's also more to Long Island than the Hamptons and the North Fork. The **Fire Island National Seashore**, a 32-mile barrier island with unspoiled beaches and the Sunken Forest, a 300-year-old holly forest, as well as an historic lighthouse you can tour. The westernmost six miles of Fire Island make up **Robert Moses State Park**, which harbors excellent beaches. And **Jones Beach** is a sun-worshipper's hot spot.

TOURIST INFORMATION

Long Island Convention & Visitors Bureau and Sports Commission, 330 Motor Parkway, Suite 203, Hauppauge, Long Island, NY 11788, Tel. 877/FUNONLI or visit www.licvb.com.

GETTING THERE

Make no mistake about it, Long Island is very much an island. Whether by car or train you'll need to get across the East River, (which separates the City from the Island) via one of seven bridges and tunnels. Note: If you plan to visit the Hamptons, you won't need, but you might want, a car once you're there because it is spread out.

By Car

Which route to take all depends on where on the Island you choose to go. If you will be traveling all the way to the Hamptons or Montauk (the very end of Long Island), your best bet is to take the Long Island Expressway (I-495) to exit 70 (Manorville). Make a right off the ramp, go to the end and make a left onto Route 27(Sunrise Highway), which will take you to the Hamptons. To get to the North Fork, take the Long Island Expressway (I-495) to Exit 73. At the bottom of the ramp you're on Route 58 to the east to Orient. The other two main express routes that cross the Island are Northern State Parkway, which runs from Queens to Hauppauge and Southern State Parkway, which runs from Brooklyn and Queens (this road is also known as the Belt Parkway) to Oakdale.

By Train

The Long Island Rail Road is the nation's largest commuter railroad. It operates 740 passenger trains daily on three major east-west routes from New York City along the entire Nassau-Suffolk County region, with 124 train stations. The LIRR offers summer package tours; call 516/822-LIRR.

WHERE ARE WE GOING NOW?

Jones Beach State Park

Ocean Parkway, Wantagh, Tel. 516/785-1600.

I grew up at the sunny beaches here and, as a travel writer now for a long time have had the privilege of traveling to some of the world's most incredible beaches: Jones Beach is right up there with the best of them.

The 2,400-acre park features six miles of ocean beach, a bayfront beach (perfect for waders), a two-mile stretch of boardwalk, an outdoor pool and a golf course. **Bonus:** The Tommy Hilfiger Theater, an outdoor theater where fabulous concerts are put on.

Splish Splash

2549 Splish Splash Drive, P.O. Box 1090, Riverhead, Tel. 631/727-3600, www.splishsplashlongisland.com, (Exit 72 West off the Long Island Expressway).

Open: Weekends from Memorial Day weekend to mid-June, then daily from mid-June to Labor Day.

Admission: Adults $34.99 (over 48 inches tall), $25.99 (under 48 inches tall and seniors 65 years and older), kids three years old and younger are free.

The largest water park in New York State, this 96-acre wonderland of water rides makes quite a splash with kids. There's a 1,300-foot-long "lazy river" ride; more than 20 water slides, including the Hollywood Stunt Rider, a totally-in-the-dark family raft ride with steep drops and surprises; a

30,000-gallon Wave Pool; Alien Invasion; Kiddie Cove; and daily performances (high dive shows, seal shows and the Great American Bird Show).

Long Island Children's Museum
11 Davis Avenue, Garden City (off Charles Lindbergh Blvd. At Mitchell Center, Exit M4 off the Meadowbrook Parkway), Tel. 516/224-5800, www.licm.org.
Open: September through June, Tuesday through Sunday 10am to 5pm; July and August daily through 10am to 5pm.
Admission: General admission $9, seniors (65 years and older) $8.
Geared for young kids (under 12 years old), this hands-on museum is

Three Hamptons Tips

• If you take the train or Jitney and plan to spend at least one night, the Southampton Inn is a great spot. The inn is centrally located in the pretty town of Southampton so you can walk to great shops and restaurants. Bonus: The inn will pick you up at the train or Jitney bus stop, and will also shuttle you to the beach. Family package prices are reasonable. For information or reservations call 800/832-6500 or visit www.southamptoninn.com.

• Oceanfront Gurney's Inn is a great Montauk getaway (not far from the Montauk Point Lighthouse—*see photo on page 156*). The property features oceanview suites, as well as a pailful of cottages and is smack on the Atlantic. In the summer there is a children's program, including things like Yoga for Kids on the beach. Bonus: The spa at Gurneys is fabulous with an indoor saltwater swimming pool that is irresistible. Located at 290 Old Montauk Hwy, 631/668-2345, www.gurneys-inn.com.

• Avoid—at all costs—driving from Manhattan to the Hamptons on Friday evenings and from the Hamptons to Manhattan on Sunday nights. The traffic on the Long Island Expressway—the most direct route—is unbearable.

fun for kids on the Island. But honestly, the children's museums in Manhattan and Brooklyn are great and there's no compelling reason to travel here to visit (unless you'll be in the area). Exhibits include things like the bubble room; a mock TV station and radio station, a hands-on Music Gallery, and a climbing structure, among others. **Bonus:** Mars Virtual Voyage Ride, $5.

Cradle of Aviation Museum
    1 Davis Avenue, Garden City, Tel. 516/572-4111, www.cradleofaviation.org
    Open: Tuesday through Sunday 9:30am to 5pm. IMAX is open seven days a week.
    Admission: $9 adults, $8 kids, IMAX movies separate admission.
    Located right next door to the Long Island Children's Museum this museum is on par with the fabulous Smithsonian Air and Space Museum in Washington, DC—but is not as large. The museum sits on the same site where Charles Lindbergh took his historic flight. In addition to really cool exhibits (especially for boys), like an F-11 Tiger and an original 1972 lunar landing module, there is an IMAX Theater with a number of aviation-and-space-related shows. **Bonus:** Junior Jet Club for ages 2 to 6 years old where kids can dress up like astronauts and blast off some steam. **Bonus:** The G-Force Encounter ride, a flight simulator experience that thrills kids.

CONNECTICUT

A compact state, Connecticut is considered to be a part of New England—but the southern part of Connecticut is a much closer sibling to New York than New England. This is because so many of the folks who live in the southern parts of the Nutmeg State work in the Big Apple. Move farther up the coast though, and there's a new chapter to the story with more evidence of New England's Puritan past. It's evident in the cuisine (lobster and chowder), in the accommodations (bed-and-breakfasts and quintessential New England inns) and in the lay of the land (sprawling town greens and a sprinkling of fishing villages).

The state's most popular tourist attraction is **Mystic Seaport**, a step-back-in-time, 19th-century village (about a two-and-a-half-hour-drive from Manhattan) where kids can board a historic ship, dress up in period clothing and hoist a sail.

We've named a couple of other family-friendly attractions in the state that are a bit closer to Manhattan for you to consider visiting, but really Mystic Seaport is where it's at for families.

Tourist Information

Eastern Regional Tourism District, 32 Huntington Street, New London, CT, 860/444-2206, www.mysticcountry.com. For Connecticut State information, call 800/CT-BOUND.

GETTING THERE
By Car

Traveling from the City by car, the most direct route is I-95. However, you'll share the road with tons of tractor-trailers and trucks. An easier route is the Hutchinson and Merritt Parkways, where rule-the-road trucks are banned. Caveat: You'll trade in trucks for deer, as this stretch of road is populated by lots of deer that are known to leap across the road—or at least attempt to.

By Train

Metro North (the New Haven Line) runs between New York City's Grand Central Terminal and New Haven; call 800/638-7646. Note: Metro North offers special excursion packages with round-trip rail service from New York City. The packages are sold by Metro North ticket agents on the day of travel at Grand Central Terminal; call 800/638-7646.

WHERE ARE WE GOING NOW?
Mystic Seaport

75 Greenmanville Avenue, Rte. 27, Mystic (exit 90 off the I-95), Tel. 888/SEAPORT or 860/572-5315, www.mysticseaport.org.

Mystic Seaport was once upon a time a proud whaling and shipbuilding center. Today, the seaport is a 17-acre, recreated 19th century seaport village whose attractions include: horse and carriage rides, boat rides and rentals, participatory plays, story-telling, sail-handling demonstrations, hands-on activities for children and the Seaport Gallery. New: Daily "Hands On History" workshops where kids can engage in activities like make a wooden boat that they take home; small fee.

We've been to Mystic many times and each time we discover something new. During our most recent trip there, on a hot July afternoon, we stumbled across a casual and funny audience-interactive performance on one of the lawn areas at the Seaport. We sat on a bench to cool off and stayed for the show.

Grab a bite to eat in the little town of Mystic at Mystic Pizza on West Main Street (Tel. 860/536-3700). This pizza joint is where Julia Roberts played her breakout role in the movie by the same name. Although it served pizza before the movie was even conceived, Ms. Roberts put this eatery on the map and it could be argued vice versa. The menu: pizza, spaghetti, hamburgers and grinders.

If you've rented a car and plan to stay more than one day (not a bad idea since it's a two-and-a-half- hour's drive, without traffic), plant yourselves at the **Inn at Mystic**, which overlooks busy Mystic Harbor and Long Island Sound; call 800/237-2415. Or, travel about a half-hour inland and spend the night at the **Mohegan Sun** (Tel. 877/204-7100, www.mohegansun.com). Of course, the kids can't gamble at this casino resort, but they'll have fun in the pool and there's a terrific kids' center they'll enjoy while you grab a bite to eat—you'll have a huge selection from which to choose.

Note: The interior of the hotel is reminiscent of a mall with tons of shops, restaurants and a couple of bars. Smoking is permitted in this "mall," and on a busy weekend, the smoke tends to linger.

The Barnum Museum

820 Main Street, Bridgeport, CT, Tel. 203/331-1104, www.barnum-museum.org.

Open: Tuesday through Saturday 10am to 4:30pm, Sunday noon to 4:30pm, closed Mondays.

Admission: $5 adults, $4 seniors and students, $3 kids (ages 4 to 17), kids under 3 years old are free.

Your kids want to join the circus? Or, are they on their way to being nominated class clown? This historical museum might pique their interest with its permanent miniature circus model and story of P.T. Barnum's life and the influence he had on 19th-century America.

Stamford Museum and Nature Center
39 Scofieldtown Road, Stamford, Tel. 203/322-1646, www.stamfordmuseum.org.
Open: Monday through Saturday 9am to 5pm, Sunday 11am to 5pm. Nature's playground is open daily, weather permitting. Heckscher Farm is open 9am to 5pm.
Admission: Adults $8, students and seniors over 17 years old $6, kids four-to-17-years-old are $4, kids under four years old are free.
A 10-acre working New England farm, visitors can participate in farm chores (woo hoo!), as well as spy interesting animals like Black Welsh mountain lambs. There are also herb and vegetable gardens and woodland trails that kids can explore.
A museum houses five galleries with exhibits depicting Native American culture, fine art and natural history. Bonus: The stars come out on the second Sunday of each month in the Planetarium. On Friday nights you can check out the solar system with a research telescope at the Observatory.

WESTCHESTER

Westchester County sits just to the City's north and is home to some of the most upscale villages and towns in the metro area. Many commuters to the City live in this neck of the woods, drawn to Westchester's tranquility and beauty.

TOURIST INFORMATION
The Westchester County Office of Tourism, 222 Mamaroneck Avenue, Suite 100, White Plains, Tel. 800/833-9282 or 914/995-8500, www.westchestertourism.com.

GETTING THERE
By Car
Westchester is about 25 miles from Manhattan, but during rush hour it will seem like a distance of 250 miles. (See individual listings for getting there by car information.)

By Train
Join the throngs of commuters who use the railways to get in and out of Manhattan each day and weekend. Metro-North has 43 station stops in Westchester on three separate lines. The railroad operates continuous

services to Grand Central Station in Manhattan. For prices and schedules call 800/METRO-INFO or visit www.mta.nyc.ny.us/mnr.

Westchester Arts Council, Tel. 914/328-ARTS, www.westarts.com. The Arts Council has information about children's concerts, theater and entertainment throughout Westchester.

Westchester County Department of Parks, Recreation and Conservation, Tel. 914/864-PARK, www.westchestergov.com/parks.

WHERE ARE WE GOING NOW?

Playland Amusement Park

Rye, New York, Tel. 914/813-7000, www.ryeplayland.org. Traveling by car from the City, take the New England Thruway (I-95) to Exit 19 in Rye. There is a parking fee. Or, purchase Metro-North's Excursion Package to Playland; Tel. 800/METROINFO, www.mta.nyc.ny.us.

Open: Call or visit the website. Open May through September.

Admission: Free. However, the rides require tickets. You can purchase booklets of tickets: the cost begins at $20. A Fun Band is $35 and is for unlimited rides for up to six hours.

Playland isn't as big as Six Flags in New Jersey, and that's part of its appeal. This Art Deco amusement park dates to 1928 and claims to be the country's first planned amusement park. It butts the Long Island Sound and includes much more than just rides and amusements. There's a beach and pool, miniature golf and many special events throughout the year including fireworks, big band concerts and puppet shows. The rides are what the kids really love and seven of the most popular rides date back to the park's original 1928 date: The Dragon Coaster, Carousel, Derby Races, Old Mill, Whip, Kiddy Coaster and Kiddy Carousel. New rides include the Crazy Mouse Coaster, Super Flight, Double Shot, Playland Plunge, Power Surge and Dream Machine.

Historic Hudson Valley

150 White Plains Road, Tarrytown, NY 10591, Tel. 914/631-8200, www.hudsonvalley.org. You can explore Sleepy Hollow Country by traveling Route 9 by car. The region is about 25 miles from Manhattan.

This region is steeped in history and there is a collection of interesting historic sites that are worthwhile exploring if your family is especially keen on learning about America's history. The picturesque area, especially the 10 mile stretch along the east bank of the Hudson River known as Sleepy Hollow Country, is a nice antidote to the city's concrete and steel landscape. Admission varies for each place, so check the website (www.hudsonvalley.org). The historic sites here include the following:

Kykuit, the Rockefeller Estate

Sleepy Hollow, Tel. 914/631-9491, www.hudsonvalley.org. See Historic Hudson Valley directions above for getting to the area.

Open: daily from May through October, except Tuesdays.

Once upon a time, this estate inspired Washington Irving's tale, *The Legend of Sleepy Hollow* (he also wrote *Rip Van Winkle)*. Today, the six-story stone estate is a part of the National Trust for Historic Preservation.

The property was originally built by John D. Rockefeller, the American philanthropist, and his son John D. Rockefeller, Jr. Yet, there is much more to Kykuit than the estate. The views of the Hudson are commanding and the gardens are works of art. One of the most celebrated gardens here is Governor Nelson A. Rockefeller's 20th century sculptures collection— think Alexander Calder, Pablo Picasso and Henry Moore. You can tour the property on your own, which we recommend because, while the guided tours are fascinating, they will not captive your children's attention.

Note: Visits to Kykuit begin at the Philipsburg Manor (see listing below) where visitors see an introductory video and then travel to Kykuit by shuttle van. You must provide a car seat for children four years old and younger for the shuttle ride. Also, note that the tours are not appropriate for children under the age of 10 years old.

Philipsburg Manor

Route 9, Sleepy Hollow, Tel. 914/631-3992, www.hudsonvalley.org. See Historic Hudson Valley directions above for getting to the area.

Open: in the summer, 10am to 5pm, daily except Tuesday. Winter hours (November and December) are 10am to 4pm, daily except Tuesday. Closed January and February. Open weekends only in March.

An 18th century farm and gristmill that was restored by John D. Rockefeller, Jr. Kids get a kick out of the oxen, cows and sheep. There is a café here that is open seasonally.

Sunnyside
West Sunnyside Lane, Tarrytown, Tel. 914/591-8763,
www.hudsonvalley.org Located just a few miles down the road from
Philipsburg Manor. See Historic Hudson Valley directions above for
getting to the area.
Open: Summer hours are 10am to 5pm, closed Tuesday. Winter
hours (November and December), 10am to 4pm, closed Tuesday. Closed
January and February. March hours, Saturday to Sunday 10am to 4pm.
Sunnyside is Washington Irving's waterfront home. Bonus: Educational children's tours are given at selected times throughout the year.

The Union Church of Pocantico Hills
Route 448, Bedford Rd., Sleepy Hollow, Tel. 914/631-8200,
www.hudsonvalley.org. See Historic Hudson Valley directions above for
getting to the area.
Open: Take a $5 tour of the church windows April through December, every day except Tuesday: Monday, Wednesday, Thursday and Friday
11am to 5pm, Saturday 10am to 5pm and Sunday 2pm to 5pm (unless
there are church activities). Closed January through March.
This church is one of the prettiest in the country. The building itself
is small and charming. Yet, what really knocks me out are the stained glass
windows by Marc Chagall and Henri Matisse, commissioned by members
of the Rockefeller family.

Van Cortlandt Manor
South Riverside Avenue, Croton-on-Hudson, Tel. 914/271-8981,
www.hudsonvalley.org. See Historic Hudson Valley directions above for
getting to the area.
Open: Summer hours, 10am to 5pm, closed Tuesday; Winter hours
(November and December), weekends 10am to 4pm. Closed January
through March.
Reminiscent of something you'd find in Colonial Williamsburg, this
18th-century complex includes a tavern, a tenant farmer's house and a
manor house. You can take a tour led by costumed guides to see open-
hearth cooking demonstrations and other examples of post Revolutionary
War ways of life. There is also a picnic area.

NEW JERSEY

Not unlike Long Island, Connecticut and Westchester, New Jersey is also home to many bedroom communities with commuters to NYC. If you are fortunate enough to have a long vacation to New York City, you might consider visiting the Garden State. But it's not "gardens" kids will want to see here. Instead, kids and families will be interested in checking out three attractions: The Liberty Science Center, Six Flags Great Adventure and Sandy Hook Gateway National Recreation Area.

TOURIST INFORMATION
New Jersey Travel & Tourism, Tel. 800/VISITNJ, www.state.nj.us/travel.

WHERE ARE WE GOING NOW?
Liberty Science Center
251 Phillip Street, Liberty State Park, Jersey City, Tel. 201/200-1000, www.lsc.org. By train from Manhattan, take the PATH train from Penn Station to the Pavonia-Newport or Exchange Place station in Jersey City. Transfer to the Hudson-Bergen Light Rail traveling toward East 22nd Street or West Side Avenue. Exit at Liberty State Park station and walk less than a block to Liberty Science Center. Time: About an hour. By car from Manhattan: Take the New Jersey Turnpike to Exit 14B. By ferry: The NY Waterway Ferry leaves from lower Manhattan; call 800/53-FERRY.

Open: Monday through Friday 9am to 5pm, weekends 9am to 6pm.

Admission: Adults $15.75, kids two-to-12 years old and seniors $11.50 and kids under two years old are free.

The Liberty Science Center has reinvented itself following an ambitious $104 million expansion and renovation project. There are tons of new exhibits worth exploring, as well as an IMAX theatre.

Six Flags Great Adventure
Route 537, Jackson, New Jersey, 732/928-1821, www.sixflags.com. By car, take the George Washington Bridge, Lincoln Tunnel or Holland Tunnel to New Jersey Turnpike South to exit 7A. Proceed to I-195 east to exit 16A, then one mile west on Rte. 537 to Six Flags. By bus: There are New Jersey Transit buses to the theme park; call 800/626-7433.

Open: Call or visit the website for updated hours.

Admission: Regular $59.99, Junior (under 54 inches) $29.99, seniors

$29.99, kids two years old and under are free. There are also combination admission deals for visiting Six Flags Hurricane Harbour and Six Flags Wild Safari; call for pricing. Budget Tip: Purchase your tickets online and the cost is $20 less, at $39.99.

This has always been the cool place to go for teens (it used to be called Great Adventures), as well as the littlest ones, thanks to tailor-sized attractions like Looney Tunes Seaport (six-acres of Bugs Bunny and friends rides and Koala Canyon, a 1/2 acre water play area).

For older kids and teens, the roller coasters are wild and will whet their appetites for rebellious fun like El Toro, a wooden rollercoaster that travels 70 mph. There are also daily shows and parades and nightly fireworks. New: The Dark Knight Coaster, a ride in total darkness.

Bonus: Right next door to this theme park is Six Flags Hurricane Harbour and Six Flags Wild Safari. Hurricane Harbour is a 45-acre complex with a million-gallon wave pool, river rides and 20 speed slides.

Six Flags Wild Safari insists it's the world's largest drive-thru safari outside of Africa. Over 1,200 animals representing species from around the globe call this safari home (giraffes, monkeys, elephants, rhinos, oh my!). Keep in mind: You'll need to have a car to cruise through the safari.

Sandy Hook Gateway National Recreation Area

National Park Service, Gateway National Recreation Area, Sandy Hook Unit, P.O Box 530, Fort Hancock, New Jersey, 07732, 732/872-0115, www.nps.gov/gate/. For information about other public transportation to Sandy Hook, call Tel. 718/354-4606 or visit www.nps.gov.

Open: The Visitor's Center is open year-round 10am to 5pm. The beach is open sunrise to sunset.

Admission: Gateway has no entrance fees. However, beach parking fees are charged at Sandy Hook (732-872-5970) during the summer.

One of the prettiest stretches of beach along the Jersey Shore, Sandy Hook also is home to the oldest lighthouse still in use (1764) and Fort Hancock. There is also a small museum here, but let's face it, New Yorkers don't escape the summer heat and make the hour-and-a-half-drive to go to a museum (not when they live in a town that's museum central). New Yorkers head here for a taste of sun and surf. There is a necklace of strands; some have bathrooms and food concessions. There are also hiking trails.

COOPERSTOWN, NEW YORK

Okay, it's a bit far—three hours from Manhattan (really though it can take that long to get to the Hamptons, too, considering summer traffic). But if you or anyone in your brood is a baseball nut then the journey from Manhattan to see **The National Baseball Hall of Fame and Museum** here must be made. End of story. Plus, the ride is pretty, through rural New York State dotted with farmland and cows and lakes. And there's more to Cooperstown than baseball. Founded in 1786 by William Cooper, father of America's first internationally known novelist James Fenimore Cooper, Cooperstown is a historical town with the country's oldest living history museum, the **Farmers' Museum** as well as **The Fenimore Art Museum**, home to an impressive collection of American art.

The Cooperstown Trolley will bring you to all the must-see places within Cooperstown.

TOURIST INFORMATION
Cooperstown Chamber of Commerce, 31 Chestnut Street, Cooperstown, NY, 607/547-9983, www.cooperstown.org.

GETTING THERE
By Car
Take the New York State Thruway to Exit 25A, take I-88 west to Exit 24, go west on Route 20, then south on Rt. 80 into Cooperstown. Once you arrive in the village of Cooperstown everything is practically within walking distance or, you can hop on and off the trolley.

WHERE ARE WE GOING NOW
Fenimore Art Museum
Tel. 888/547-1450, www.fenimoreartmuseum.org.
Open: mid-April through mid-May 10am to 4pm Tuesday through

Sunday, closed Monday; mid-May through Columbus Day weekend open 10am to 5pm daily; mid-October through December open Tuesday through Sunday 10am to 4pm.

Admission: Adult $11, seniors $9.50, kids seven years old to 12 years old $5, kid six years old and under are free.

A showcase for American art collections of The New York State Historical Association, including folk art and James Fenimore Cooper memorabilia. My son particularly enjoyed the separate wing that houses American Indian art. But make no mistake, this is not children's museum by any stretch of the imagination and your kids will last only so long. A pretty outdoor café overlooks Otsego Lake, a perfect spot for lunch.

The National Baseball Hall of Fame

Tel. 888/425-5633, www.baseballhalloffame.org

Open: Memorial Day through Labor Day 9am to 9pm daily. Otherwise, open 9am to 5pm daily.

Admission: $16.50 adults, $11 seniors, $6 kids ages seven to 12 years old. Kids six and under are free.

Home Base: The Otesaga!

The grande dame of Cooperstown is The Otesaga Resort with its sprawling porch and rockers, from which guests admire the views of Otsego Lake in the distance. The resort has been around since 1927 and is a Cooperstown centerpiece with its stately columns and brick façade. Golfers appreciate the championship, 18-hole Leatherstocking Golf Course and foodies appreciate the kitchen—the food is wonderful. At the Hawkeye Bar & Grill, watch a game as we did with

former Hall of Famers sitting at the adjacent table. A thrill for any baseball fan. Call 800/348-6222 or visit otesaga.com.

If you love baseball you won't want to leave this museum devoted to the game and a showcase for more than 150 years of baseball history. My son and I were thrilled to find information in the Hall of Fame's re- search library about my great-grandfather Con Daily, a major league catcher and his brother Ed Daily, a major league pitcher. There was even information about my son's father when he was a minor leaguer with the New York Yankees. The museum is home to the bronze plaques of 260 Hall of Fame members, artifacts from historic ballparks and a 19th-century exhibit. There's also a well-done multimedia show. Thirty team lockers, one for each major-league club, contain artifacts from the best players in the game today. Kids enjoy the hands-on activities at the Sandlot Club House.

There are tons of special events and activities throughout the year. We recently visited the Hall of Fame during a commemorative celebration of the Brooklyn Dodger's only championship in 1955 and had a wonderful time rubbing elbows with some of the players from that team like Robin Roberts, Johnny Podres and Carl Erskine. Call or visit the website for more information about special events.

New: Kids (nine years old and older) and their parents can now sleep overnight here right in the Hall of Fame Plaque Gallery. Cost: $49.95 adults, $39.95 kids. For more information about the sleepovers, call 607-547-0312.

The Farmers' Museum

Tel. 888/547-1450, www.farmersmuseum.org.

Open: mid-April through mid-May Tuesday through Saturday, closed Sunday and Monday; mid-May through Columbus Day 10am to 5pm daily; the rest of the month of October open Tuesday through Sunday only; Thanksgiving weekend open Friday and Saturday 10am to 4pm; and open in December one weekend for a candlelight evening.

Admission: $9 adults, $8 seniors (65 years and older), $4 for children ages 7 to 12 years old, free for kids six years old and under. Off-season admission is $7.50 adults and kids ages 7 to 12 years old are $4.

Kids adore this interactive museum reminiscent of Mystic Seaport and Sturbridge Village but much smaller and more intimate. The 1840's recreated village houses the American Paper-Staining Manufactory, the only working block press wallpaper workshop open to the public in North America. But what kids really like is roaming the grounds, watching the cows being milked, shopping in the General Store, visiting the heritage gardens and petting the animals at the Children's Barnyard. We loved it here.

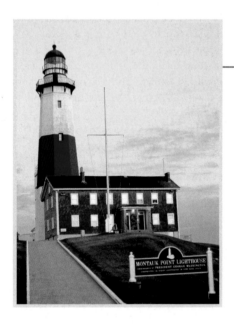

15. PRACTICAL MATTERS

CLIMATE & WEATHER

New York City typically experiences Mother Nature's four seasons, although some years the city ducks the extreme winter and summer temps it is eligible for.

The winters can be frosty cold and snowy—or, mild and snow-free. If you find yourselves in a New York City snowstorm, rejoice! The pace in this hustle-bustle town almost comes to a halt and New Yorkers celebrate the event. You'll even see them cross-country skiing down Broadway.

Spring is a special time in the city but the weather can be finicky and rainy; some springs are downright cold.

Summers in New York are almost always humid and can sometimes be unbearably hot. The city is prone to heat waves and by day two or three of one of these spells the subways and streets can be insufferable. Still, unlike many European cities, there is plenty of opportunity to cool off in air-conditioned restaurants, cafes and stores.

Fall is glorious in the Big Apple. Cool days and crisp nights usher in a new season of Broadway plays, university students and the hustle-bustle of office workers whose summer vacations are mere memories.

Here are the average yearly temperatures in New York City. However, keep in mind that there is nothing average about New York and the temps tend to fluctuate higher or lower:

* January   26 (L)   38 (H)
* February   27 (L)   40 (H)
* March   34 (L)   49 (H)
* April   44 (L)   61 (H)
* May   53 (L)   72 (H)
* June   63 (L)   80 (H)
* July   68 (L)   85 (H)
* August   67 (L)   84 (H)
* September   60 (L)   77 (H)
* October   50 (L)   66 (H)

- November   41 (L)   54 (H)
- December   31 (L)   42 (H)

WHAT TO PACK

Pack for the season. Your woolies and warmest coats and boots if you'll be visiting in the winter (November through March). Spring is tough: days can warm up but nights cool down so you'll need to layer. Travel here in the summer and your suitcases will be light—shorts, T-shirts, sundresses are all you'll need. Also pack a bathing suit if you decide to escape the heat and head for Long Island's beaches—or if your hotel has as swimming pool.

New York is a casual town. Shorts, jeans, T-shirts, sandals and sneakers, anything goes. If you will be going to the theater pack a city-chic outfit. There are only a handful of restaurants where he'll be required to wear a jacket and tie (and chances are you won't be dining at those with children).

STROLLERS & BACKPACKS

New York is a walking town and you'll definitely need a stroller if you've got young kids. Some of my fondest memories of living in Manhattan are taking walks with my son in a stroller. Good news: Most museums allow strollers (although you won't be permitted to bring a stroller into every exhibit within the museum). If you have an infant, pack along a snuggly and keep him or her tucked in front of you. I know a lot of parents love those backpack contraptions that they put their kids into and they're great in some situations. However, in a city setting, I preferred to see my young son in front of me so I could keep on eye on him.

ARRIVALS & DEPARTURES
Making Plane Reservations

Thanks to the Web, finding competitive airfares is a cinch. But the choices can be dizzying and airfares change faster than a New York minute.

General rule of thumb: The further out you book the lower the fare. As soon as you know of your children's school vacation schedules try to plan your flights. There is a handful of good websites to tap. Expedia (www.expedia.com), Travelocity (www.travelocity.com) and Orbitz (www.orbitz.com) are good options. Consider flying into a secondary airport (in the case of New York, that would be MacArthur on Long Island or Westchester Airport, both of which are served by major airlines). If you can, be flexible with dates. Although not as convenient, it's amazing how drastic the fare can be depending on the date. Of course, you can also visit a specific airline's flight to check out deals and even book your flights. Or call the airline and ask for promotional rates. Connecting flights are usually cheaper but can be tough on families flying with young children. Travel agents can be an invaluable resource. A good agent will have preferred-supplier deals with several airlines. You can still surf the Web for good deals. Then, let the agent know of the deal you found and see if he or she can match it or beat it.

Tip: When booking your flight try to determine which side of the airplane will afford fliers with the best skyline view (your travel agent or airline agent may be able to help). Flying over and into Manhattan is a tremendous experience—especially for kids. Fly at night and the city appears as a magical place; during the day it's still a formidable presence. Also, inquire about the best seats at the gate when you arrive at the airport. See if you can change your seats accordingly if it's determined that there will be better views from the other side of the plane. Remember to smile and pour on the charm and your request might be granted.

Three major airports serve New York City. They are:

John F. Kennedy International Airport (JFK) in Queens, Tel. 718/244-4444, www.panynj.gov JFK serves primarily international flights, although some domestic flights have arrivals here, too. It is about an hour's drive into midtown Manhattan—*without* traffic.

Fiorello LaGuardia Airport (LGA) in Queens, Tel. 718/533-3400, www.panynj.gov LaGuardia serves primarily domestic airlines and is the shortest ride into Manhattan—about 35 minutes *without* traffic

Newark Liberty International Airport (EWR) in Newark, New Jersey, Tel. 973/961-6000, www.panynj.gov Newark serves domestic and international carriers and is about an hour's drive into Manhattan—*without* traffic.

There are two other metropolitan-area airports:

Westchester Airport (HPN) in White Plains, Westchester, New York, Tel. 914/995-4860, www.westchestergov.com/airport.

MacArthur Airport (ISP) in Ronkonkoma, Long Island, New York, Tel. 631/467-3210, www.macarthurairport.com.

Here is a sampling of some of the major airlines that serve the New York metropolitan area.
• Delta 800/221-1212, www.delta.com
• American 800/433-7300, www.aa.com
• America West 800/235-9292. www.usairways.com

- Continental 800/525-0280, www.continental.com
- Jet Blue 800/538-2583, www.jetblue.com
- United Airlines 800/241-6522, www.united.com
- Southwest Airlines 800/435-4322, www.southwest.com
- Virgin Atlantic 800/862-8621, www.virgin-atlantic.com
- US Airways 800/428-4322, www.usairways.com

FROM LAGUARDIA TO MANHATTAN

To travel from LaGuardia Airport to midtown Manhattan consider the following children-and-luggage-friendly options:

Taxi

Tel. 212/NYC-TAXI.

The easiest—and most affordable way—to travel from the airport to Manhattan is by taxi. One fare covers all the passengers in the cab. The metered fare is: $21 to $30 plus bridge and tunnel tolls and tip (the driver usually pays the tunnel or bridge fare at the crossing and then adds it to the final fare). Note: Look for uniformed airport agents who drive yellow medallion taxis. If you follow the signs marked "Ground Transportation" while you exit the airport you'll ultimately find the taxi stand.

Super Shuttle

Tel. 888/888-6025, 212/BLUE-VAN.

Cost: $13 to $22 one way to midtown Manhattan

This van will deliver you right to your hotel—but you're not saving money by taking a bus rather than a taxi because a taxi charges per family or load, while the bus charges per person. Still, if you opt for the bus, as you exit the baggage area, go to the Ground Transportation Desk. The van makes stops at all of the major hotels between 23rd and 96th streets. Caveat: You may have to wait at the airport but it's not usually more than 20 minutes. Note: When returning to the airport from your Manhattan hotel, you must make reservations for your pickup 24 hours in advance.

FROM JFK TO MANHATTAN

Taxi

As when traveling between New York City and LaGuardia, a yellow medallion taxi is your easiest and most cost-effective bet. As you exit the airport, follow the signs marked "Ground Transportation." Accept rides only from uniformed airport agents. One fare covers all passengers. The fare is $45 flat-fee (non-metered) plus bridge and tunnel tolls and tips.

AirTrain JFK
> Tel. 212/435-7000, www.airtrainjfk.com.

This is an inexpensive way to get to and from Manhattan to JFK ($5 each passenger; children under 5 are free) but it's certainly not the most convenient way. The light rail service makes a 1.8 mile (8 minute) loop linking the nine airline terminals, as well as a 3.3 mile extension with stops at employee parking and long term lots, terminating at Howard Beach subway where you catch the A train (subway) for the ride into Manhattan. Or, you can take it another 3 miles into the Jamaica station and transfer to the Long Island Railroad or the E, J and Z subway lines or a dozen bus lines. Yes, it's a cheaper service but it's not kid-and-luggage friendly by any stretch of the imagination.

FROM NEWARK TO MANHATTAN
Taxi

As when traveling from LaGuardia and JFK, a taxi is the most cost-effective and easiest way to get from Newark International Airport into the City.

Terminal A Taxi: City of Elizabeth Taxi and Limousine Commission, Tel. 908/820-4178. Cost: between $50 and $70, plus tolls and tips. There is a $1 charge for each piece of luggage.

Terminals B and C Taxis: City of Newark Taxi and Limousine Commission, Tel. 973/733-8912. One fare covers all passengers: the fare ranges between $50 and $70, plus tolls and tips to midtown Manhattan. There is a $1 charge for each piece of luggage over 24 inches.

AirTrain Newark
> Tel. 888/EWR-INFO.

This new, regional rail transportation connects Newark International Airport to Manhattan's Penn Station (33rd Street and Seventh Avenue). Do not follow signs for "Ground Transportation;" instead, look for signs marked "Monorail/AirTrain Link." You can take the AirTrain directly from the arrivals terminal to the Rail Link station and then connect with NJ Transit or Amtrak for rail travel into Penn Station. AirTrain is a free service, but the NJ Transit fare between Newark Airport Station and New York's Penn Station is $15.

FROM WESTCHESTER AIRPORT TO MANHATTAN
Taxi/Private Car
Tel. 914/592-8534 or 877/878-5466..

When you exit the airport look for the signs marked "Ground Transportation." The Limousine Service of Westchester provides by-demand taxi and limo service. Seek out a company representative at the Ground Transportation desk. Cost: $100-$125 including tolls and tip.

Bee-Line Bus Systems Bus
Tel. 914/813-7777.

This bus line provides service between the airport and the White Plains train station, at which point you can transfer to a Metro-North train into Grand Central station in midtown Manhattan. The bus service is $2 per person, the Metro-North train is about $7 per person (pay no more than $1 for each kid, ages five-to-11-years-old with a fare paying adult; not valid on inbound morning commuting trains). A half-price child fare applies to the fifth child. Kids five years old and under ride free.

FROM MACARTHUR AIRPORT TO MANHATTAN
Shuttle Van and Train
Colonial Transportation (Tel. 800/464-6900) provides shuttle service between the airport and the Ronkonkoma train station (10 to 12 minute ride), where you can hop aboard a Long Island Railroad train into NYC's Penn Station. Shuttle buses run every 15 to 20 minutes and cost $5 per person (kids eight years old and younger are free). At the airport's entrance (yes, there's one main entrance; it's a small airport), look for a white van marked "Express service between Islip/MacArthur Airport and LIRR/Ronkonkoma Train Station." The train ride is about 1 hour and 20 minutes and the cost is $6.50 to $9.50 depending on whether you'll be traveling at peak times (translation: rush hour). Kids ages five-to-eleven-years-old ride half price; kids five years old and under ride free.

By Private Car & Limo
Nothing beats the convenience of a private car or limo service from the airport to your hotel. Here is a handful of companies that serve all of the metro airports. You can expect to pay about $65 from LaGuardia, $75 from JFK, $80 from Newark and between $100 and $125 from Westchester and MacArthur airports. Note: You must reserve in advance.
- Colonial Transportation, Tel. 800/464-6900
- Carey Limousine NY Tel. 800/336-4646
- Executive Town Car & Limousines, Tel. 800/716-2799

By Train

There are two main train stations in New York City—**Pennsylvania Station** (on the West Side) and **Grand Central Station** (on the East Side). Amtrak trains come into both stations, depending on their origin. Penn Station is a final destination for Amtrak's Northeast Corridor routes, including Washington, DC and Boston, MA. This is a great way to travel to New York, and many families do. The route from Boston and points south to New York is especially pretty as it hugs the coast. Kids 2 years old to 15 travel half-price with an adult; children under 2 years old travel free (not valid on the weekday Acela Express and Metroliner). Student and senior discounts are also offered, and Amtrak offers rail passes available for international travelers. Amtrak also offers train, hotel and attraction packages. Call 800/872-7245, www.amtrak.com.

By Car

You won't need—nor want—a car in New York City and if you can get here another way, ditch the car idea. It's expensive to park your car in Manhattan (garage rates average $40 per day) and you won't need it to explore the city and outer boroughs anyway. At all costs, avoid driving into the city at rush hour and on Sunday afternoons in the summer when New Yorkers return from their summer homes in the Hamptons and other leafy or sandy spots. From points north and south, I-95 will take you to New York City, from points west, take I-80. For detailed directions, visit www.mapquest.com or contact AAA if you're a member.

PUBLIC HOLIDAYS

The City That Never Sleeps gets some shuteye on holidays. But it doesn't enter the REM stage. While offices, government buildings and banks close, many museums and theaters stay open, but check individual listings in the book.

The holidays are:
- January 1, New Year's Day
- Third Monday in January, Martin Luther King Day
- Third Monday in February, President's Day
- Last Monday in May, Memorial Day
- July 4, Independence Day
- First Monday in September, Labor Day
- Second Monday in October, Columbus Day
- November 11, Veteran's Day/Armistice Day
- Last Thursday in November, Thanksgiving
- December 25, Christmas

SPECIAL EVENTS

In a city as big and diverse as New York, there are special events held every day, from festivals to parades to concerts. For more information about any of them, visit www.nyc.om. Here is a sampling of the major events:

January
• Martin Luther King Day
• National Boat Show at the Jacob Javits Center

February
• Black History Month
• Abraham Lincoln's Birthday
• Chinese New Year Celebrations (*see photo below*)

• George Washington's Birthday
• New York Yankees Fan Festival
• Westminster Kennel Club Dog Show

March
• St. Patrick's Day
• Ringling Bros. And Barnum & Bailey Circus

April
• Macy's Flower Show
• Central Park Easter Egg Roll
• Fifth Avenue Easter Parade
• Earth Day Celebrations
• Major League Baseball Season Begins
• National Tartan Day Celebration

May
• Cherry Blossom Festival, Brooklyn Botanic Garden
• Tribeca Film Festival
• Memorial Day

Summer (June, July, August)
• Museum Mile Festival (*every second Tuesday in June, rain or shine*)

- National Puerto Rico Day Parade, Upper East Side
- JVC Jazz Festival New York
- Shakespeare in the Park at the Delacorte Theater
- Central Park SummerStage
- New York Philharmonic Concerts in the Park
- Bryant Park Film Festival
- Fleet Week
- South Street Seaport Fourth of July Festival
- Macy's Fourth of July Fireworks
- Lincoln Center Out-of-Doors Festival
- Harlem Week
- Midsummer Night Swing at Lincoln Center
- Mostly Mozart Jazz Festival
- U.S. Open Tennis Tournament
- National Puerto Rican Day Parade
- Lesbian and Gay Pride Parade

September
- West Indian American Day Parade, Labor Day
- Feast of San Gennaro in Little Italy
- New York is Book Country Festival
- The New York Film Festival

October
- Greenwich Village Halloween Parade
- New York Rangers Hockey season begins
- New York Knicks Basketball season begins

November
- New York City Marathon
- Veteran's Day Parade
- Thanksgiving Day Parade

December
- Kwanzaa Fest
- Lighting of the bigger-than-life Chanukah Menorah at Fifth Avenue and 59th Street
- Lighting of the Rockefeller Center Christmas tree
- New Year's Eve at Times Square, ball-dropping countdown

GETTING AROUND ON YOUR OWN

There are five boroughs in New York City—the Bronx, Brooklyn, Manhattan, Queens and Staten Island. A lanky necklace of bridges and tunnels links the five boroughs.

Manhattan is an island, flanked on the West Side by the Hudson River and on the East Side by the Harlem River (to the north) and the East River (to the south). North of Manhattan is the Bronx, which is on the mainland. The boroughs of Queens and Brooklyn are located on the western tip of Long Island.

The island of Manhattan is 13.4 miles long and 2.3 miles wide at its widest point.

The streets run east to west and are numbered, ascending in numerical order traveling north from Houston Street all the way up to 220th Street. The streets south of Houston Street have their own names. On average, 20 north-south blocks equal a mile.

Avenues run north to south, beginning with 1st Avenue on the East Side and ending with 12th Avenue on the West Side. Note: Sixth Avenue is also called Avenue of the Americas. The East and West sides of Manhattan are divided by Fifth Avenue. The farther you travel from Fifth Avenue the higher the numbers; there are roughly 100 street addresses per block.

Broadway is the only avenue that cuts diagonally through the city and runs in some form from Manhattan's southern tip all the way to the state capital, Albany, about 150 miles away.

The city is sectioned into regions.

- Anything below 1st Street in Greenwich Village is considered **Downtown**.
- The area between 1st and 14th Streets is considered **The Village**. The neighborhood west of Broadway is considered Greenwich Village and the neighborhood east of Broadway is considered the East Village.
- The area between 14th and 34th Streets, west of Broadway, is known as **Chelsea**.
- Between 34th and 59th Streets is **Midtown**.
- From 59th to 110th Streets is where you'll find the **Upper West Side** and the **Upper East Side**. Between the two "sides" lies **Central Park**.
- The neighborhood between 110th and 145th Streets is **Harlem**.
- The area between 145th to 220th Streets contains the neighborhoods of **Washington Heights**.

Generally speaking, the traffic patterns are as follows: one-way going east on even-numbered streets and one-way going west on odd-numbered streets. Main streets that run east west are two-way yet some of the smaller streets are the exception to this rule.

Orient yourself further by logging onto www.nycvisit.com to download maps. Or, visit one of the visitor information kiosks located throughout town. And keep in mind, that New Yorkers are friendly and love to share their knowledge of the City with tourists. Don't be shy—just ask.

By Car

Are you kidding? You don't want to get behind the wheel to drive around the city. End of story.

Car Rental

Again, you won't need—or want—a car to explore the city, however you may want to rent one to explore the suburbs. Here is a listing of car rental agencies in Manhattan.

• Dollar, Tel. 800/800/3665, www.dollar.com
• Budget, Tel. 800/527-0700, www.budget.com
• National, Tel. 800/227-7368, www.nationalcar.com
• Hertz, Tel. 800/654-3131, www.hertz.com
• Enterprise, Tel. 800/736-8222, www.enterprise.com
• Avis, Tel. 800/917-2847, www.avis.com

By Subway & Bus

A whopping 3.5 million people rely on New York's subway and bus system on a daily basis. Many of the subway and bus lines operate 24 hours a day. The fare is $2, even if you're only going one stop—it is the same as if you're taking it to the end of the route.

You'll need a **MetroCard** to use the subway, but you can also use change for the buses. Best bet: Purchase an unlimited-ride card for one day (the Fun Pass $7), seven day card ($24) or, if you'll be in town for an extended vacation (lucky you) a 30 day care ($76). You can buy pay-per-ride cards in increments of $2 to $80. If you buy a pay-per-ride card worth $10 or more, you get a 20 percent bonus. Note: You can use your Metrocard for free transfers between buses and subways or bus-

-to-bus within two hours of the ride's start. You can buy MetroCards at any subway station, hotels, and newsstands throughout the city. You can also purchase a MetroCard at NYC's Official Visitor Information Center.

Note: The subway is safe and reliable—but you should stay away from the subway late at night and opt to take a cab or bus instead.

By Taxi

How to hail a cab: Standing at the curb (on the sidewalk,) simply hold your arm out and wave. (Kids love to do this but make sure they stay on the

curb). You can hail a yellow taxi on any street or at taxi stands at most major hotels. Look for the middle section of the taxi's roof light to be on. If it's not, and the off-duty lights are on (on each end of the light) or, if no part of the light is lighted, the taxi won't stop because it already has another passenger or is off-duty. Tip: Hail a cab that is headed in the direction you want to go. Also, make sure it is a yellow taxi; if it is not, you risk being overcharged.

By Water Taxi

You can circumvent the congested New York streets and jump aboard a bright yellow water catamaran taxi instead. The 74-passenger-capacity taxis zip along the rivers serving neighborhoods, parks and attractions along the West Side, Lower Manhattan and Downtown Brooklyn waterfronts. Bonus: There's even a café onboard. A one-way ticket (if you'll be going one way for more than one stop) costs $10 adults, $6 seniors and kids 12 years old and younger. Bonus: Buy a one-day pass, which allows you to hop on and off New York Water Taxi at any time during a 24 hour period for $20 adults, $15 seniors (65 years and older) and kids (12 years old and under). Two-day passes are also available.

Note: Children two years old and under ride free. Note: Babies in baby strollers are allowed; strollers with no babies are not. You can purchase tickets aboard the boats, at one of the kiosks (seasonal) and at some of the landing docks. Note: No winters season service. For more information, call 212/742-1969 or visit www.nywatertaxi.com.

GETTING AROUND BY ORGANIZED BUS TOURS
Gray Line New York Sightseeing/Coach USA

Tel. 800/669-0051 or 212/445-0848, www.newyorksightseeing.com. Kids and adults love the double-decker bus tours—you can jump on and off as you please for two consecutive days. Gray Line recently introduced The History Channel's Official NYC Heritage Tour, a daily, hop on and off trolley tour that takes visitors through a journey in time as it visits many famous New York sites. Guides in period costume relive such New York monuments as George Washington bidding farewell to his officers during the Revolutionary War. Also new is a Taste of New York City tour. Budget: Buy online and receive a buy one, get one free deal.

Showbiz Insiders Tour

Tel. 800/669-0051 or 212/445-0848 (Reservations are required, you can also buy them online). www.newyorksightseeing.com.

A Gray Line tour of the country's hit television and Broadway productions, this tour allows star-struck visitors a chance to meet a Rockette at Radio City Music Hall. After a lunch at Planet Hollywood in Times Square, the tour culminates with a performance by a current Broadway actor at Gray Line New York Sightseeing's private theater, Blue Diamond. Bonus: Opportunities for autographs and photographs with the stars.

Harlem Spirituals/New York Visions

Tel. 212/391-0900 or 800/660-2166, www.harlemspirituals.com.

Gospel music and jazz are part of this company's MO. Tours are offered of Manhattan, the Bronx and Brooklyn.

Harlem Your Way! Tours Unlimited

Tel. 800/382-9363, www.harlemyourwaytours.com.

General tour of Harlem (jazz, gospel, architecture, and churches), as well as customized tours, including special children's tours.

Shop Gotham Shopping Tours

Tel. 212/209-3370, www.shopgotham.com.

One of the Big Apple's newest tours, this tour is designed for your teenager daughter who loves to shop.

On Location Tours, Inc.

Tel. 212/209-3370, www.sceneontv.com.

Calling all couch potatoes. Grab a seat on one of these bus tours of famous TV and movie sites. You can choose from the following:

Manhattan, TV and Movie Tour, which includes *Friends, Ghostbusters, Spiderman* and *You've Got Mail; Sex and the City* Tour, including 35 spots in the series, such as Carrie's apartment; *The Sopranos'* Tour, which features 40 sites; and the Central Park Movie Tour, which covers 60 locations.

Kramer's Reality Tour

Tel. 800/KRAMERS, www.kennykramer.com.

Seinfeld is the quintessential New York story and this three-hour coach bus tour takes a behind-the-scenes look.

GETTING AROUND BY BOAT

Circle Line Sightseeing Cruises

Pier 83, West 42nd Street and 12th Avenue, Tel. 212/563-3200, www.circleline42.com.

Circle Line is one of the city's most established lines to operate cruises around Manhattan. There is a three-hour narrated Full Island Cruise, which is not the one you want if you have small kids or impatient teens (ahem). The two-hour Semi-Circle Cruise or evening two-hour Harbor Lights Cruise (the skyline at night is a jewel to behold) is a better bet.

Even better though for kids, is the *Beast*—a 30-minute thrill ride that is not for the faint of heart. This boat, which departs from Pier 83 at West 42nd Street, zips along the river and kids adore it! For information about the *Beast*, visit www.infocl@circleline.com. Note: Kids must be over 40 inches tall or five years old. Cost: From mid-May to the end of September, open daily, noon to dusk; Adults $18, kids (12 years old and younger) $12. Note: During the month of October open only on Saturday and Sunday. The boat departs every hour on the hour.

Circle Line also operates the new Circle Line Statue of Liberty Ferry/*Zephyr*, a luxury catamaran of Battery Park. 212/269-5755, www.zephyrcruises.com. There's a kid-friendly, one-hour narrated tour of just the Statue of Liberty and Ellis Island Immigration Museum.

Chelsea Screamer

Tel. 212/924-6262, www.chelseascreamer.com.

This boat zips along the East River past the Brooklyn Bridge, the Statue of Liberty, Ellis Island, up to the *Intrepid* and back. The trip takes about 30 minutes. We had such a good time on this ride that we made plans to take my mother on the boat the following week. She reminded us that she takes Dramamine for canoe rides and we decided this wasn't the cruise for her. Or for anyone in your family if they're prone to seasickness. The boat travels at a good clip—about 45 mph. Our guide was a scream, cracking jokes while dishing up important and trivial facts about the City. The *Screamer* is for kids ages of all ages, while the *Beast* (see Circle Line tours) is better suited for teens. Operates weekends June through October.

Cost: Call for hours and cost. Pier 62 at Chelsea Piers (West 23rd Street and Hudson River).

Staten Island Ferry

Tel. 718/876-8441, www.siferry.com.

A great way to see the Manhattan skyline, New York Harbor and the Statue of Liberty—for free. The ferry runs 24 hours a day between St. George on Staten Island and Whitehall Street in Manhattan. The five-mile trip is about 25 minutes each way. More than 60,000 passengers use the ferry each day.

NY Waterway Baseball Cruises

Tel. 800/533-3779, www.nywaterway.com.

Hit a home run with the baseball nut in your family with this cruise to Yankee Stadium. Bonus: Packages are available, including tickets to games. Round-trip fares are $22 adults, $18 kids under 12, free for kids three years old and younger.

GETTING AROUND BY WALKING TOURS

ARTime

Tel. 718/797-1573.

Kid-friendly tour for kids in the range of five to ten years old. Tours run seasonally. Call for more information.

Museum Adventures

Tel. 212/794-2867, www.museumadventuresnyc.com.

For kids (and their parents) tours that include visits of museums throughout the city. Each tour culminates with an art activity.

Big Onion Walking Tours
Tel. 212/439-1090, www.bigonion.com.

Year-round tours of New York's historic districts and ethnic neighborhoods led by "smart" tour guides (the company insists they all hold advanced degrees in American history or related fields), and are licensed by the city. The annual Christmas Eve stroll through Greenwich Village is magical and includes a reading of *'Twas the Night Before Christmas.*

Central Park Conservancy
Tel. 212/360-2726, www.centralparknyc.org.

You can choose from eight different walking tours of Central Park. The tours span woodlands and meadows, bridges and waterways and offer snippets of info about Central Park's history and design. Highlight: One-hour tours written and led by NYC teens. Bonus: All tours are free. No reservations required.

Cityhunt Urban Adventures
Tel. 877/HUNT-FUN, www.cityhunt.org.

Think scavenger hunt and you get the picture.

Joyce Gold History Tours of NYC
Tel. 212/242-5762, www.joycegoldhistorytours.com.

Bus and walking tours that skip along with interesting commentary of the city's history and architecture, a Joyce Gold tour is one of the City's most popular tours. Ms. Gold is a fountain of information. Note: These tours are geared primarily toward adults and older teens.

Grand Central Terminal Tours
Tel. 212/883-2420, www.grandcentralterminal.com.

Two free walking tours are offered of this magnificent terminal building. On Wednesdays, the Municipal Arts Society runs a tour; meet at 12:30 pm at the information booth on the Grand Concourse (212/935-3960). On Fridays, a tour is conducted by the Grand Central Partnership; meet at 12:30 pm in front of the Sculpture Court of the Whitney Museum of Altria on East 42nd street, across from the terminal (212/883-2420). (For more specific information about Grand Central Station, check out the separate listing in the midtown section of the book).

Toro Associates, Inc.
Tel. 212/625-9977, www.chinatowninfo.com.

A $15 walking tour that gives you a sneak peek into Chinatown's historical landmarks, herbal medicine stores and jade and crystal shops.

Big Apple Greeter
Tel. 212/669-8159, www.bigapplegreeter.org.
Explore Manhattan for free with volunteer guides who'll meet you at your hotel or wherever you want and give you an intimate peek at the city (any borough)—by foot, subway or bus. The tours generally run two-to-four hours. Over 500 New York volunteers are trained to lead these guides; tours are conducted in over 22 languages. Bonus: All tours are free and there is a no tipping policy. Note: Reserve at least a month in advance.

GETTING AROUND BY BIKE TOURS
Bite of the Apple Tours/Central Park Bike Tours
2 Columbus Circle/Broadway at 59th Street, Tel. 212/541-8759, www.centralparkbiketour.com.
Leisurely two-hour bike rides through Central Park. Bonus: If your kids love the movies, sign up for the Central Park Movie Scenes Bike Tour. Cost: $40 adults, $20 kids 15 years old and under. Budget Tip: Reserve online and receive a 10 percent discount.

Bike the Big Apple
Tel. 201/837-1133, www.bikethebigapple.com.
These five-to-seven hour cycling tours take visitors over bridges, on quiet, ethnic streets and places not generally seen on traditional tours. Yes, kids take these tours—there's a guide to lead the group and a guide following. The pace is slow and all skill levels participate. You can also customize a tour for your family: Tours include bicycle and helmet. Prices vary depending on tour.

GETTING AROUND BY AIR
Helicopter Flight Services
Tel. 212/355-0801, www.heliny.com.
Don't forget your cameras for the fabulous aerial views. The 13-to-15-minute New Yorker Tour soars over the Statue of Liberty, Empire State Building, and *Intrepid* Aircraft Carrier. Cost: $129 per person.

Liberty Helicopters, Inc.
Tel. 212/967-6464, www.libertyhelicopters.com.
Five-to-seven minute tours that sweep over The Empire State Building, the *Intrepid* and Central Park. Cost: $75 per person.

PLAYGROUNDS, PARKS, GARDENS & RECREATION

New York City has more than 1,700 parks, playgrounds and recreation areas in five boroughs. Here is a sampling of some of the best of them; you'll undoubtedly stumble across others on your own.

NATURE CENTERS, PARKS & GARDENS

Battery Park City Parks Conservancy (BPCPC)

2 South End Avenue, Tel. 212/267-9700, www.bpcparks.org.

Roughly 32 acres dotted with playing fields and playgrounds make the parks and gardens along this stretch the pride and joy of downtown Manhattan. Designed and maintained (without the use of toxic chemicals) by celebrated landscape architects and artists, Battery Park also contains more than two-dozen art installations, four museums and several restaurants. Shadowed by soaring skyscrapers, this is the spot for free weekly recreation, art and sports activities for kids of all ages during the spring, summer and fall months. Wagner Park, located north of Battery Park, is a perfect place here to spy the Statue of Liberty and Ellis Island.

Rockefeller Park, also part of the BPCPC, is a sliver of a park, with wide expansive lawns for hanging and picnicking with a little bit of everything within a gated area: a sculpture garden for kids, a wading pool, a playground and a carousel. There's also a stretch of grass to picnic on and an esplanade for biking and rollerblading. The playground is particularly popular. On a hot day kids can run through elephant and hippopotamus sprinklers. There are several sand play areas, and a huge net, rope and chain bridge. Of course there are the requisite swings and you can also rent board games, ping pong paddles, jump ropes and balls at the Park House. For older kids there's a basketball and handball court.

East River Park

Along the FDR Drive, beginning at Montgomery Street up to 14th Street.

A park for sports enthusiasts with fields for soccer, football, softball and baseball. Bonus: Great views of the East River, the Brooklyn and Manhattan bridges.

Central Park

See chapter 10.

Brooklyn Botanic Garden
See pages 90-91.

Staten Island Botanical Garden
1000 Richmond Terrace (Tysen Street to Snug Harbor Road), Staten Island, Tel. 718/273-8200, www.sibg.org.
Open: Dawn to dusk daily.
Admission: Free. Chinese Scholar's Garden $5 adults, $4 students, seniors and kids 12 years old and under. Connie Gretz Secret Garden, open Tuesday through Sunday, 10m to 4pm, $2 adults (free if accompanied with a kid).
There are 50 acres with 25 gardens on the grounds of the Snug Harbor Cultural Center. The Chinese Scholar's Garden has lovely reflecting pools and meditation courtyards.

Queens Botanical Gardens
See pages 85-86.

New York Botanical Garden
Bronx River Parkway, Bronx, Tel. 718/817-8777, www.nybg.org. (Take Metro North out of Grand Central Station).
Open: Tuesday through Sunday and holidays, 10am to 6pm (November through March open until 5pm). Closed Monday except holidays.
Admission: As prices vary and change frequently, it's best to call. Note: Free admission Saturday 10am to noon, and all day Wednesday (grounds only admission.)
A 250-acre paradise in the Bronx, this jewel is a National Historic Landmark. It boasts 27 outdoor gardens and plant collections and the Enid A. Haupt Conservatory, a Victorian conservatory with a huge 90-foot-high glass dome. The Everett Children's Adventure Garden, 12 acres of gardens and wetlands, will make any kid a green thumb with hands-on plant discovery activities; there's also a picnic area.

Flushing Meadows-Corona Park
See page 85.

Riverbank State Park
145th Street (at the Hudson River), Tel. 212/694-3600, www.nysparks.com.
Open: Seven days a week, 6am to 11pm.

Admission: Free.

A 28-acre oasis near Columbia University, Riverbank has a pedestrian esplanade, as well as a carousel (open only on Saturdays and Sundays during warm weather months; 50 cents). There are also tennis courts, an outdoor ice-skating rink and an Olympic-sized indoor pool. Note: No bicycles allowed.

PLAYGROUNDS

You could argue that New York City is a giant playground for people of all ages and countries and you'd be right. There are tons of fun diversions and activities. But for the purposes of this section, we're talking the sandy type of playgrounds for kids under 12 years old.

Some of these playgrounds are located in parks with benches that lure office workers to enjoy their lunch—making for a complete New York scene. For instance, on a pretty day, the Madison Square Park Playground located in the shadows of the Flatiron building, is a magnet for the stroller crowd, as well as professionals with their sleeves rolled up, ties tucked in, munching on lunch.

There are way too many playgrounds to list in these pages. Here is a listing of some of the best, strategically placed play spots to swing, slide and chill:

- West 67th Street Playground, North of Tavern on the Green
- Heckscher Playground, West 62nd Street
- Diana Ross Playground, West 81st Street (Central Park—*see photo below*)

- Hudson Street Playground
- West 84th Street Playground
- Spector Playground, West 85th Street
- Safari Playground, West 91 Street
- Tompkins Square Park, Avenue A and 7th Street and Avenue B and 10th Street
- Wild West Playground, West 93rd Street
- Pat Hoffman Friedman Playground, East 79th Street (Central Park)
- Pier 51 Playground at Horatio Street

RECREATIONAL ACTIVITIES

Basketball

New York is a hoops town and you'll see pick-up games all around town. Even if your kids don't live for the game, you'll want to spend at least a couple of minutes at "The Cage," basketball courts at Sixth Avenue and West 4th Street. You'll know you arrived by the crowds of onlookers watching the action with mouth-gaping awe. We've spent several summer evenings licking ice cream cones while admiring these hoopsters in action. Some of the kids who play pick-up games here are serious NBA contenders. Yes, your kids can join in but they'd better be good.

A wiser bet for joining a pick-up game: St. Catherine's Playground on First Avenue between 67th and 68th Streets. Or, if you're milling about the Great Lawn in Central Park (around 85th Street), they might be able to get in on the action at the nearby courts.

Parent Tip

Combine a visit to the Metropolitan Museum with the Ancient Playground East, 85th Street and Fifth Avenue. Fashioned after the Egyptian Wing of the Metropolitan Museum, which is located next door, this popular outdoor spot is one of the few playgrounds that doesn't just cater to the diaper crowd. Rope and tire swings, pyramids and a chain-link bridge entertain older kids, while bucket swings and a sandbox engage younger kids. (Don't let them dig too deep, they might just excavate a mummy.) Teens might like the chess and checker tables.

Biking

Central Park is fun for cyclists of all ages—if your last name is Knievel. Seriously, you must be alert to dodging in-line skaters, joggers and oblivious strollers. You can rent bicycles mid-park at the Loeb Boathouse.

The most family-friendly stretch is along Riverside Park, thanks to its relatively flat and wide paths from about 83rd street up to 96th.

You can also bike over the Brooklyn Bridge which is really cool—just be sure to stay in the bike "lanes"; pedestrians have their own lane, but these lanes are not clearly marked, there's little signage and things can get dicey.

The Hudson River bike path is ambitious, spanning from Battery Park at the southern tip of Manhattan all the way up to the George Washington Bridge. Caveat: There are some stretches along the way that are difficult to maneuver, especially way uptown.

Parent Tips

If your kids are sports-enthusiasts, they'll most likely want to jump, run, hit and slam-dunk while on vacation. But you certainly don't want to lug basketballs, tennis rackets and baseball bats to town. Don't sweat it. You have several choices:

• At Central Park's **North Meadow Recreation Center**, located mid-park at 97th Street, there are handball courts, indoor and outdoor climbing walls, basketball courts and a fitness learning center and you can borrow equipment (with ID) like Double Dutch jump ropes. Call 212/348-4867 ext. 10, www.centralparknyc.org

• Chelsea Pier Field House (Pier 62 at Chelsea Piers) is another hot spot for athletic kids. You can rent playing time on a basketball court or slug baseballs in the batting cage. (See chapter 5 for more information.)

Bowling

For bowling-loving families, there are a couple of popular bowling spots in town, but they're probably considerably more expensive than bowling in your hometown.

Bowlmor Lanes: 110 University Place (between 12th and 13th streets), Tel. 212/255-8188, www.bowlmor.com. Cost: Sunday through Thursday before 5pm, $9.45 per person per game, Friday and Saturday before 6pm and all-day Sunday $9.95 per person per game (nobody under 21 years old is allowed at night). A hip, happening, date-night spot that's family-friendly during the day with 42 lanes, automatic scoring and gutter bumpers to keep the balls from going astray.

300 New York at Chelsea Piers: Located between Pier 59 and 60 at West 23rd Street and the Hudson River, Tel. 212/835-2695, www.chelseapiers.com. Cost: Monday through Friday $8 per game per person daily, plus $6 shoe rental per person; weekends a little higher. After 9 pm, anybody 21 years old and under must be accompanied by an adult. New York families love to bowl here. It's clean and has gutter bumpers. Bonus: You can order food from the restaurant and they'll deliver it to your lane.

Leisure Time Bowling: 625 Eighth Avenue (in the Port Authority Bus Terminal) on the second level, Tel. 212/268-6909, www.leisuretimebowl.com. Cost: $6.50 per person, per game weekdays before 5 pm; other times $9.50 per game. Shoe rental is extra. Even seasoned New Yorkers will look at you as if you have ten heads if you ask for directions to the bowling alley in the Port Authority Bus Terminal. Tell them it really exists—on the second level, with 30 lanes and kids bumper bowling.

Hiking

New York is about as flat as you can get, so don't expect much in the way of mountainous treks. Still, you can "hike" through parts of Central Park (see chapter 10). We're guessing that you didn't come to New York in search of expert hiking. For that, you'll want to head to Westchester, New Jersey or Connecticut.

Golf & Miniature Golf

Clearview Park Golf Course: 202-12 Willets Pt. Blvd. (Clearview Expressway), Queens, Tel. 718/229-2570, www.americangolf.com. One of the most popular public courses in the metro area, this 8-hole course also affords golfers views of the Long Island Sound.

Dyker Beach Golf Course: 86th Street and Seventh Avenue, Brooklyn, Tel. 718/836-9722 www.americangolf.com. A public, 18-hole golf course, with views of the Verrazzano Narrows Bridge.

Golf Club at the Chelsea Piers: Pier 59 at Chelsea Piers, 23rd Street and the West Side Highway (at the Hudson River), Tel. 212/336-6400, www.chelseapiers.com. A four-level, driving range that accommodates 52 golfers at one time. Bonus: Stunning Hudson River views (great sunsets) and heated stalls for year-round play. Works like a baseball hitting range: a computerized system in the floor spits a new ball up onto your tee immediately after you've smacked the previous one. The complex also houses a 1,000-square-foot practice putting green. Need lessons? Pros are also available.

Randall's Island Family Golf Center: Randall's Island (drive across the Triborough Bridge or take the shuttle bus from 86th Street and Third Avenue), Tel. 212/427-5689. Sports are what this no-frills, non-manicured park under the auspices of the Triborough Bridge are all about, and there is a miniature golf course here. You'll also find lively cricket matches, soccer games and flag football. Sometimes, a big event like a concert or, the Cirque du Soleil, will take place on this Island. But for the most part, it's where kids and adults play team sports. However, there are big plans underway for a 26-acre water park to be built here so stay tuned.

Ice Skating/Roller Skating

The Rink at Rockefeller Center: Fifth Avenue (49th and 50th), Tel. 212/332-7654, www.therinkatrockcenter.com. The queen of all ice skating rinks, to lace up and skate here is a quintessential New York City experience. Bonus: Skate during Christmastime when the lighted tree towers over the rink and your hearts will sing. Caveat: The rink is small and the holiday season is the busiest time in the city so plan it right—come when it first opens—or, be prepared to wait a long time in outdoor lines and to share the ice with the crowds.

Nice touches: The rink is usually lined with tourists who enjoy the amateur show. The *Today Show* studios and plaza is a snowball throw away. In summer, the rink doesn't transform into a roller-skating rink like many other rinks. Instead, it becomes a lovely outdoor restaurant. For a short time in spring, a tent is draped over it and it becomes the scene for a spectacular orchid display. For information about admission and hours, call or visit the website.

Trump Wollman Rink (*see photo below*): Enter north of the Park entrance at 59th Street and 6th Avenue, Tel. 212/439-6900, www.wollmanskatingrink.com. This outdoor ice skating rink has several

things going for it. It's in Central Park with a midtown location, it affords skaters with great skyline views (at night is especially dramatic when it's all-aglow) and it's teen heaven—rock music is piped in. There are restrooms and a casual snack bar for the requisite hot cocoa. Bonus: In the summer, Victorian Gardens at Wollman Rink Amusement Park takes over. For information about admission and hours, call or visit the website.

Bryant Park: Between 40th and 42nd streets, www.bryantpark.org. Bryant Park is flooded to become an ice skating rink each winter. Not as crowded as Rockefeller Center and less expensive (free admission), it's a perfect spot to twirl figure eights. Note: The rink closes up early in the winter season to get ready for Fashion Show Week.

Sky Rink at Chelsea Piers: Pier 61 at Chelsea Piers, 23rd Street, Tel. 212/336-6100, www.chelseapiers.com. Admission and hours: Call or visit the website for more information. Challenge: Your Sarah Hughes-wannabe-daughter loves to ice skate but you'll be visiting New York in the middle of the summer. Enter Chelsea Piers, an ambitious sports complex with twin, year-round, indoor skating rinks. General skating time sessions are usually held in the afternoons and some evenings; call of check for updated schedules. Bonus: Views of the boats slipping by on the Hudson River give you a sense of place.

SPECTATOR SPORTS

Brooklyn Cyclones

Keyspan Park, 1904 Surf Ave. (West 17th-19th Streets), Coney Island, Brooklyn, Tel. 718/507-TIXX, www.brooklyncyclones.com.

The Class-A Mets Minor League Baseball team slugs here at Keyspan Park with the Coney Island Ferris wheel a home run hit away. You can reach the Park by Subway: Take the Q local, W, F, or N train. The last stop on those trains is the Stillwell Avenue/Coney Island station. Exit the station towards Stillwell and Surf Avenues; the Park is two blocks away.

New York Giants & New York Jets

Meadowlands Sports Complex, The Meadowlands, East Rutherford, Tel. 201/935-3900, www.meadowlands.com.

New York's two football teams, the New York Giants and New York Jets, play at this sprawling, $450 million sports complex. For information about the Giants, call 201/935-8111. For information about the Jets, call 516/560-8100. To get to The Meadowlands, you can take a bus (it's a 20-minute ride) from the Port Authority terminal; round-trip bus service for all events is offered. Advanced-purchased ticket is required and tix are hard to come by; call 800/772-2222 for more information.

New York Knicks

Madison Square Garden, 2 Penn Plaza (7th Avenue between 31st and 33rd Streets), hotline Tel. 212/465-JUMP, www.thegarden.com.

One of the hottest tickets in town is a Knicks' ticket (especially if they're having a good season, which has not been the case lately). Knicks games are a ton of fun and there are usually celebs sitting courtside (Spike Lee, Woody Allen)—no matter how their team is doing.

New York Liberty

Madison Square Garden, 2 Penn Plaza (7th Avenue between 31st and 33rd Streets), Tel. 212/564-WNBA, www.nyliberty.com.

Women's professional basketball team that puts on a good show and that you have a chance of getting tickets to one of their games.

New York Mets

Shea Stadium, 1223-01 Roosevelt Avenue (126th Street), Flushing, Queens, Tel. 718/507-TIXX, http://newyork.mets.mlb.com.

See listing on page 88.

New York Rangers

Madison Square Garden, 2 Penn Plaza (7th Avenue between 31st and 33rd Streets), Tel. 212/307-7171, www.newyorkrangers.com.

New York's professional ice hockey team play a ton of games here (mostly at night) during the season. Tickets to a Rangers game, however, can be as difficult to score as to a Knicks game.

New York Sharks

Shark Field at the Aviator Sports Complex Brooklyn, Tel. 646/552-5790, www.nysharksfootball.com.

Professional Independent Women's Football League.

New York Yankees

Yankee Stadium, 161st Street (River Avenue), Bronx, Tel. 212/307-1212, www.yankees.com.

See listing on pages 94-96.

Staten Island Yankees

Richmond County Bank Ballpark at St. George (adjacent to Staten Island Ferry Terminal), Staten Island, Tel. 718/720-9265, www.siyanks.com.

This New York Yankees minor league affiliate showcases Yankees prospects in a cool stadium that overlooks New York Harbor. You can get to the Ballpark by Subway: Take the 4 or 5 subway to Bowling Green or the N or R to the Whitehall Station, then hop on the Staten Island ferry (it's free). Exit the ferry from the lower deck and the ballpark is to your right. Note: The ferry departs every 15 minutes on weekdays between 5 and 7pm, and every 30 minutes on weekends until 7pm and 60 minutes thereafter. For more information about the ferry (including the holiday schedule), call 718/720-9265.

Billie Jean King National Tennis Center

Flushing Meadows-Corona Park, Tel. 866/OPEN-TIX, www.usopen.org.

Tennis lovers know that this Tennis Center is home to one of four

Grand Slam professional tennis events. The Center is located across the way from Shea Stadium. In fact, to get to the Center from Manhattan by train, you'll take the take the #7 subway to the Shea Stadium/Willets Point Station. The Tennis Center is a quick walk down the ramp from the station.

THEATERS

New York is home to 39 Broadway theaters and more-than-you-can-count off-Broadway and off-off Broadway theaters. For an up-to-date listing of current Broadway shows and theater addresses, go to www.playbill.com. Here are some kids' theaters and theaters that show occasional children's productions:

The Theater at Madison Square Garden

Seventh Avenue (between 31st and 33rd Streets), Tel. 212/307-1000, www.thegarden.com.

The Christmas Carol is staged here each holiday season, as is the Ringling Bros. and Barnum & Bailey Circus and concerts.

New Victory Theater for Kids and Families

209 West 42nd Street (between Broadway and 8th Avenues), Tel. 646/223-3020, www.newvictory.org.

The New Victory is all about theatre for kids and families. All kinds of performances are produced here, including dance, comedy, theater and puppetry. Bonus: The price is right: Orchestra seats are $24.50, mezzanine seats are $17.50 and balcony seats are $8.75. There are also VicTeens (kids 11 to 18 years old) performances. Even the concession stands here won't break your budget; items like pretzels, cookies and raisins run $1 to $3.

York Theater at Saint Peters in Citicorp Center

Citicorp Center, Lexington Avenue at 54th Street, Tel. 212/935-5824.

This small theater sometimes produces kid shows, as well as adult shows.

AMC Loews IMAX Theatre at New York City

Sony Theatres at Lincoln Square, 1998 Broadway at 68th Street, Tel. 212/336-5020, www.bigmoviezone.com.

There are a gazillion movie theaters around town, some showing kids movies, others featuring low-budget flicks. This 75-foot-high/97-foot-wide screen theatre is in a class of its own. Films are scheduled on a rotating basis.

There's a smaller, albeit not much smaller (everything being relative), IMAX theater at The Museum of Natural History. (see listing under Museums section).

TADA! Youth Theater

15 West 28th Street (between Broadway and Fifth Avenue), Tel. 212/252-1619, www.tadatheater.com. Tickets: General admission tickets are $18 adults, $8 kids 15 years old and under.

The MO here is "by kids for kids." Actors ages 8 to 17 stage musicals so exciting they've been invited to perform at the White House. Nice touch: Restless kids can sit on bench seats.

TELEVISION TAPINGS

There are lots of television shows taped in the Big Apple and many of these programs invite audiences for free.

Note: Some of these shows you'll need to reserve your free seats weeks or months ahead of time so plan accordingly. Sometimes, though, standby tickets are available on the day of taping. (If you're willing to pay, go to www.newyorkshow.com and they'll help you secure tickets.)

Also, keep in mind that not all shows allow kids at tapings. Here is a sampling of shows:

Late Night with Conan O'Brien

NBC Studios, 30 Rockefeller Plaza, 50th Street at Sixth Avenue, Tel. 212/664-3056, www.nbc.com.

Late Night With Conan O'Brien tapes Monday through Friday at 5:30 pm. Ticket reservations are accepted in advance only by calling the NBC ticket office at the above number or online. Advance reservations are limited to four tickets per group. Note: Kids must be 16 years old and older.

The Daily Show with Jon Stewart

Daily Show Studios, 733 11th Avenue, (51st and 52nd streets), Tel. 212/586-2477, www.dailyshow.com.

Kids under 18 aren't allowed to this Comedy Central show, but perhaps you can trade off with your spouse. Stewart and his sidekicks are hilarious. This is my favorite show on television—and has been my son's since he was a pre-teen. My opinion is that, if not totally appropriate at all times, this show is generally speaking fine for teens to watch. In fact, newspaper and television accounts of the same news stories often include gory, graphic pictures that are far more disturbing than Stewart's comic takes. The show tapes every Monday through Thursday at 5:45 pm. To request free audience tickets to attend a live taping, you must visit the Comedy Central website at www.comedycentral.com.

Live with Regis and Kelly

ABC Studios, West 66th Street between Columbus Avenue and Central Park West, Tel. 212/456-3054, www.tvplex.go.com/buenavista/livewithregis.

Caveat: There is a one year wait for snail mail tickets, but you can often snag same-day tix; arrive at the corner of 67th Street and Columbus Avenue around 7am to request a standby number. Standbys are seated if there are remaining seats after ticketholders have been seated. Children under 10 not admitted.

To order tickets in advance by mail, send a postcard to: *Live with Regis and Kelly Tickets*, Ansonia Station, P.O. Box 230-777, New York, NY 10023-077.

Saturday Night Live

30 Rockefeller Plaza, 50th Street (at 6th Avenue), Tel. 212/664-3056. www.*nbc.com*.

"Live from New York, it's Saturday Night Live." This is a tough ticket to snag thanks to its popularity. To enter the lottery, send an e-mail in the month of August to snltickets@nbcuni.com. You must be 16 years old. To get standby tickets for the dress rehearsal or the show, arrive at 7am at 49th Street and 30 Rockefeller Plaza on mornings of tapings. One ticket per person, first-come, first-served.

The View

ABC Studios, 320 West 66th Street, www.abc.abcnews.go.com/theview/main.html.

To get free tickets in advance, go to *The View's* website and click on tickets. *The View* airs live Monday to Friday from 11 am to noon; arrival time is 9:30 am.

There is also a handful of live television shows with sidewalk studios that you don't need tickets for. Here's a sampling:

The Early Show

Fifth Avenue at 59th Street, www.cbsnews.com.

Housed in the General Motors Building at Trump International

Plaza, you can watch the morning news show action on this ground level set through huge glass windows. Tapings are 7am to 9pm.

Good Morning America

Times Square (44th Street and Broadway), www.abcnews.go.com.

Wake up with the hosts of *Good Morning America* as they present this morning news show. The show airs every weekday from 7am to 9am. You can go inside the studio; for tickets fill out the form at the Website.

The Today Show

30 Rockefeller Plaza, Fifth to Sixth Avenues, www.nbc.com.

The Today Show started the trend of sidewalk studios a couple of years ago. Sneak peeks at Meredith Vieira and Matt Lauer while they do this morning news show inside the studio on the ground floor at the corner of 49th Street and Rockefeller Center. The cameras often pan the crowd—to better your chances of being seen stand on the southeast corner—behind the anchor desk. *The Today Show* airs on weekdays between 7am and 10am.

MOVIE SHOOTS

New York is extremely photogenic and has been the setting for many Hollywood blockbuster films and popular television shows. To get an up-to-date listing of movies or television shows currently being shot in the Big Apple, visit the Mayor's Office of Film, Theatre and Broadcasting's website at www.nyc.gov/film or call 212/489-6710.

PERFORMING ARTS
Carnegie Hall

154 West 57th Street (7th Avenue), Tel. 212/247-7800, www.carnegiehall.org.

Ask a New Yorker on the street how to get to Carnegie Hall and they'll tell you to take the N, Q or R trains... ask my son and he'd say "practice, practice, practice." Alex has performed two piano solos here (in a recital with other children). Of course, Carnegie is also the stage for celebrated artists from all over the world. Alex's piano teacher is one of them—the famous pianist, Dr. Maria Botazzi. There are also fabulous kids' programs, including:

Saturday-afternoon Family Concerts, for kids age 5 to 12 years old. Cost: $9, including pre-concert activities and a child-friendly concert. Each child gets a copy of *KidsNotes*, an age-appropriate performance program.

CarnegieKids, for kids ages 3 to 6 years old, is held each spring and fall. Pre-schoolers get jazzed with these 45-minute concerts that are a mix of music and storytelling and motivate kids to get up and sing and dance. Cost: $6. Advance reservations are recommended.

Lincoln Center for the Performing Arts

Columbus Avenue between 62nd and 66th streets, Tel. 212/875-5350, www.lincolncenter.com.

This sprawling complex is home to several of the City's most important theaters. They are The Metropolitan Opera House, Avery Fisher Hall, Alice Tully Hall and NY State Theater. Everything from opera to dance to the symphony is performed here. **Bonus:** A tree at Christmas is decorated *a la* performing arts with trumpets and other musical instruments.

Also at Lincoln Center is the **New York City Ballet,** formerly the American Ballet Theater. When Mikhail Barishnikov danced with ABT I'd buy partial-view seats (cheap tix) and see every performance he danced.

Then, I'd wait outside the stage door to catch a glimpse of him which, sadly, I never did. Misha no longer dances with the company but the New York City Ballet still puts on fabulous productions nonetheless, including *Swan Lake* and *Don Quixote.*

Parent Tip

After much anticipation, Jazz at Lincoln Center has finally moved into its new home at the AOL Time Warner Center at Columbus Circle to become the world's first performing arts facility devoted to jazz. The impressive center is perched high above Central Park, with bandstands posed against towering walls of glass. Called the Frederick P. Rose Hall, the facility features two theaters, a jazz club, a recording studio, several classrooms and the Ertegun Jazz Hall of Fame. The Hall of Fame is a multi-media installation with interactive kiosks, projection screens and audio components. **Bonus:** Admission is free to all visitors of the hall.

Celebrated trumpet player **Wynton Marsalis** hosts a series of family concert series such as "What is Jazz Piano" and "What is the Blues?" Ticket run between $12 and $32. You can reserve them at the Alice Tully Hall box office on 65th Street or by calling CenterCharge, 212/721-6500.

BAM (Brooklyn Academy of Music)

30 Lafayette Avenue (between Ashland Place & St. Felix Street), Tel. 718/636-4100, www.bam.org.

BAM is not about Emeril. BAM is home to contemporary and unique opera, dance, music, theatre, film and new media. There are several theatres here: the Howard Gilman Opera House, the Harvey Theater and BAM Rose Cinemas. BAM has tons of kid stuff throughout the year, including events like the annual BAMkids Film Festival and BAMfamily Book Brunch.

The Amato Opera Theatre

319 Bowery (close to 2nd Street), Tel. 212/228-8200, www.amato.org.

Kid-friendly (shorter than the standard) operas-in-brief performances are staged here in this intimate theater. Think *Hansel and Gretel*, and you get the idea.

The Joyce

175 Eighth Avenue (at 19th Street), Tel. 212/242-0800, www.joyce.org.

An intimate theater for fabulous avant-garde and modern dance performances.

Alvin Ailey American Dance Theater

405 West 55th Street and 9th Avenue, Tel. 212/405-9020, www.alvinailey.org.

The largest facility devoted exclusively to dance in the country, The Joan Weill Center for Dance opened here with a 300-seat theatre, as well as 12 dance studios for the Alvin Ailey Dance Company.

Tribeca Performing Arts Center

199 Chambers Street, Tel. 212/220-1460, www.tribecapac.org.

Family Folk & Fairytales, a downtown family performing arts series of classic children's tales set to music, with puppetry and acrobatics. Kids ages 3 to 10 years old. Tickets cost $25 for kids and adults.

GETTING TICKETS

For Madison Square Garden events and big theatre productions:

• Ticketmaster, Tel. 800/755-4000, www.ticketmaster.com

• TeleCharge, Tel. 800/432-7250, www.telecharge.com

• Madison Square Garden, Tel. 212/307-7171, www.thegarden.com

For same-day tickets for off-Broadway and Broadway shows head to the **TKTS booth**, run by the Theatre Development Fund (212/221-0885, www.tdf.org). There are two TKTS locations. In midtown, there is a TKTS booth at Duffy Square (47th Street and Broadway). Hours: Monday through Saturday 3pm to 8pm for evening performances; Wednesday and Saturday 10am to 2pm for matinees; and Sunday 11am to 8pm for matinees and 3pm to closing for evening performances.

Downtown, there is a TKTS booth at South Street Seaport at John and Front Streets (the rear of the Resnick/Prudential Building at 199 Water Street). Hours: Monday through Saturday 11am to 6 pm; Sunday 11am to 3:30pm. Many of the tickets are sold at half price, others are discounted at 25% (keep in mind that half price sounds great, but full ticket prices are sky high so it'll still cost you.) Note: You must pay in cash or with traveler's checks; credit cards are not accepted. And, there's a service charge tacked on. The lines at the TKTS booths can be extremely long (hours)—certainly not for youngsters. The uptown booth is centrally located in the thick of the Times Square action and kids will be preoccupied with the big city

Free Performances in the Parks!

If you are in town during the summer months, you won't want to miss one of the city's most delicious cultural pleasures—free performances in the parks. For info about some of the free outdoor performances, visit the Central Park Conservancy at www.centralparknyc.org, or call the New York Parks and Recreation Hotline, Tel. 888/NYPARKS. Here's a sampling of some of the best of them:

• The New York Philharmonic, Tel. 212/875-5656, www.newyorkphilharmonic.org

• The Metropolitan Opera, Tel. 212/362-6000, www.metopera.org

• The Public Theater's Shakespeare in the Park, Tel. 212/539-8500, www.publictheater.org, lights, as well as the street performers and taxis whizzing by (you're on an island in the middle of Broadway). Or, have one parent take the kids to the nearby Toy's 'R Us Ferris wheel or ESPN Zone while the other parent buys the tickets.

You can also get tickets by visiting the box office window of the show you'd like to see. Bonus: The box offices don't charge service fees. Even if a show is sold-out, arrive at the box office early in the day to inquire about rush tickets—last minute or returned or unsold seats. You might even end up with box seats!

You can also pick up discount coupons for many shows at NYC's Official Visitor Information Center, 810 Seventh Avenue at 53rd Street, 212/484-1222. Hours: Monday to Friday 8:30 am to 6pm, Saturday and Sunday 9am to 5pm.

Another option but it'll cost you: Ask your hotel concierge if they can help you secure theater tickets. Many concierges can spin magic; remember to tip.

Before you arrive in town, there are a number of ways you can get tickets to shows.

Go to the NYC & Company's website, www.nycvisit.com, and check out the Special Offers section and the Broadway page. Also visit the Visitor Section, click on "Services" in the left-hand column and choose "Ticket Services." Bonus: If you sign up for the site's Visitor page you'll receive a monthly e-mail newsletter called "NYC This is Your City," filled with information about discounts on theater, hotels and attractions.

RESOURCES
Miscellaneous
Live Broadway: www.livebroadway.com.
The Theatre Direct International: www.broadway.com
Applause Theater & Entertainment Ticket Service: www.applause-tickets.com
TheaterMania: www.theatermania.com
Alliance of Resident Theatres: www.offbroadwayonline.com
Communications for the Parks Department (Special Events): Tel. 888/NY-PARKS
Moviefone: Tel. 212/777-FILM
Lincoln Center Events: Tel. 212/LINCOLN

Publications
Once you're in the Big Apple, there are excellent publications you

should get your hands on that can be helpful to you while visiting. Some are distributed to hotel rooms. They include the following:

Time Out New York
Time Out New York Kids
WHERE Magazine
City Guide Magazine
IN New York Magazine
The Big Apple Parent
The Village Voice
New Yorker
New York Magazine
New York Observer

The New York Times weekend section (published on Friday) is full of happenings in the City's museums, theatres and attractions.

BUDGET TIPS

Several of the museums and attractions in Manhattan have a "pay what you wish" policy in effect all the time (although they suggest admission prices), while others offer the policy during designated evenings. Here is a sampling of museums with a "**pay what you wish**" policy and the days/times this rule applies. (Note: For more detailed information about these museums and attractions, check out the listings in the appropriate chapters).

- The Metropolitan Museum of Art and The Cloisters (www.metmuseum.org, 212/535-7710). The suggested admission is $20 for adults, $15 seniors and children. However, what most people don't realize is that a "pay what you wish" policy is in effect *every* day.
- The Solomon R. Guggenheim Museum (www.guggenheim.org, 212/423-3500). The museum offers free admission on Fridays between 5:45pm and 7:45pm.
- The American Museum of Natural History (www.amnh.org, 212/769-5100). There is a *suggested* admission, however, every day is "pay what you wish."
- The Museum of the City of New York (www.mcny.org, 212/534-1672). The *suggested* admission is $20 for families, $9 adults, $5 seniors, students and children. The museum is free on Sundays between 10am and noon.
- The National Museum of the American Indian (www.nmai.si.edu, 212/514-3700). Admission is free.
- The New Museum (www.newmuseum.org, 212/219-1222). The museum offers free admission on Thursdays between 7pm to 10pm.

- The Museum of Modern Art (www.moma.org, 212/708-9400). Admission is free Fridays from 4pm to 7:45pm.
- Whitney Museum of American Art (www.whitney.org, 800/WHITNEY) Pay-what-you-wish admission is Fridays from 6pm to 9pm.
- Jewish Museum (www.thejewishmuseum.org, 212/423-3200) Pay-what-you-wish admission is Thursdays from 5pm to 8pm.
- Forbes Magazine Galleries (www.forbesgalleries.com, 212/206-5548) Admission is free.
- The New York Hall of Science offers free hours of admission that vary considerably throughout the year. (For specific dates and hours, visit www.nyhallsci.org, 718/699-0005).
- The Bronx Zoo has a pay-what-you-wish admission policy on Wednesdays.
- The Staten Island Zoo has a pay-what-you-wish admission policy on Wednesdays after 2pm.
- Museum of Jewish Heritage—A Living Memorial to the Holocaust is free on Wednesdays between 4pm and 8pm

BASIC INFORMATION
Hospitals
- Columbia-Presbyterian Medical Center, 168th Street and Broadway, 212/305-2500
- Mount Sinai Medical Center, 98th Street and 5th Avenue, 212/241-6500
- New York Hospital/Cornell Medical Center, 70's and York, 212/746-5454
- New York University Medical Center, 34th Street and 1st Avenue, 212/263-7019
- Memorial Sloan-Kettering Cancer Center, 68th Street and York Avenue, 212/639-2000
- St. Vincent's Medical Center, 11th Street between 6th and 7th Avenues, 212/604-7000
- St. Lukes-Roosevelt Hospital, 115th Street and Amsterdam, 212/523-4000

All-Night Pharmacy
Call 800/748-3243 for listings of 24-hour pharmacies in the City.

Police
The number for police headquarters is 646/610-5000. In the event of an emergency, call 911.

Safety & Security

Ironically, since the September 11 terrorists attacks, New York City was recently named safest big city in the country according to an FBI report. That's remarkable. Still, you should be aware of your surroundings and be street savvy.

Some tips: Avoid desolate streets at night. Avoid Central Park at night. Don't carry a purse that does not have a zipper and carry it close to your body. I would also not recommend backpacks to carry infants and young babies; instead, carry your infant in front of you so you can see him or her at all times. Never leave your child in an unattended stroller—anywhere. Not only is it dangerous, it's illegal to do so. If you have older teens and are okay about giving them some space, buy a couple of walkie-talkies or, at the very least, a cell phone so you can be in contact with them.

In efforts to deter terrorism from striking New York City, you'll see heavy police presence at strategic locations including Grand Central Station, Penn Station and the Statue of Liberty. You can also be certain of tons of behind-the-scenes security and police, including radiation detectors, and bombproof garbage cans.

Security is beefed up, of course, at the New York City airports. You should anticipate waits at check-in, so arrive at the airport early.

Note that many New York City attractions do not allow you to enter with backpacks or packages, including Yankee Stadium, Shea Stadium, Madison Square Garden.

Visitor's Information & Help

There are several NYC & Company kiosks around town. They are:

New York City's Official Visitor Information Center: 810 Seventh Avenue, between 52nd and 53rd Streets, Tel. 212/484-1222. Hours: Monday to Friday 8:30am to 6pm; Saturday, Sunday and holidays 8:30am to 5pm; Thanksgiving, Christmas and New Year's 9am to 3pm. Subway: Take the B, D, E to Seventh Avenue (and 53rd Street); N, R, S, Q to 57th Street; or 1 to 50th Street. This is the city's official visitor's center where you can pick up free brochures and discount coupons to attractions and theater. There's also a MetroCard vending machine, an ATM machine and multilingual visitor information counselors.

NYC Heritage Tourism Center: Located at the southern tip of City Hall Park on the Broadway sidewalk at Park Row. Hours: 9am to 6pm, Monday through Friday and 10am to 6pm Saturday and Sunday. Subway: The 1 and 2 to Park Place; the N, R, 4, 5 or 6 to Brooklyn Bridge/City Hall; the A, C to Broadway/Nassau Street; the E to WTC/Chambers; or the J, M, Z to Fulton Street. Operating as the visitor gateway to Lower Manhattan, the kiosk features a multilingual staff who can give visitors directions, attraction brochures, event listings, maps and more.

Harlem Visitor Information Kiosk: Located at Adam Clayton Powell State Office Building plaza, 163 West 125th Street, east of Adam Clayton Powell Jr. Boulevard (Seventh Avenue). Hours: Monday through Friday 9am to 6pm, Saturday and Sunday 10am to 6pm. Subway: A, B, C, D, or 2, 3 to 125th Street. One of the newest kiosks, the fact that there is now an information center in Harlem now speaks volumes about the neighborhood as a tourist attraction.

Official Visitor Information Kiosk for Chinatown: Located at the triangle where Canal, Walker and Baxter meet. Hours: Sunday through Friday 10am to 6pm, Saturday 10am to 7pm. Subway: N, R, Q, 6, J, M, Z to Canal Street.

Other places to get tourist information:

The Alliance for Downtown New York: 120 Broadway, Ste. 3340 (between Pine and Cedar streets), Tel. 212/566-6700, www.downtownny.com. Open: Monday through Friday 8am to 5:30pm. Brochures and guides and maps are yours for the asking here. You can also get tons of info on the website.

Brooklyn Tourism & Visitors Center: Brooklyn Borough Hall, 209 Joralemon Street (between Adam and Court streets), Brooklyn, Tel. 718/802-3846, www.brooklyn-usa.org. Open: Monday through Friday 10 am to 6 pm. Information, brochures and maps about Brooklyn.

Grand Central I Love NY Booth: Grand Central Terminal main concourse, East 42nd Street (at Park Avenue), Tel. 212/340-2210, www.grandcentralterminal.com. Visit the centrally located info booth with questions or take a free tour.

Times Square Alliance: 1560 Broadway (between West 46th and West 47th streets), Tel. 212/869-1890, www.timessquarealliance.org. Open: Daily 8 am to 8 pm. One-stop shopping for Metro Cards, maps, tours, you can even surf the Web.

Wall Street Rising Downtown Info Center: 55 Broad Street (at Exchange Place), Tel. 212/425-4636, www.wallstreetrising.org. Open: Daily Monday through Friday 9am to 5pm. Information center for lower Manhattan.

READING LIST

Enrich your children's visit to New York City by encouraging them to read about the Big Apple—before they arrive or during their trip. New York plays a central role in many children's fiction books, and there are also non-fiction books that can be informative.

A friend of mine, Camille Purcell, is a respected librarian and mother of elementary-school children Miranda and Henry. Here are Camille's recommendations for great New York City reads.

Fiction

Miffy Loves New York City, Dick Bruna, Big Tent Entertainment (Ages 4 to 8)

The Adventures of Taxi Dog, Debra Barracca, Sal Barracca and Mark Buehner, Puffin, New York (Ages 4 to 9)

Uptown, Bryan Collier, Henry Holt and Company (Ages 4 to 8)

Milly and the Macy's Parade, Shana Corey, Scholastic Press, New York City (Ages 6 to 8)

Central Park Serenade, Laura Godwin, Joanna Cotler (Ages 4 to 8)

Snow White in New York, Fiona French, Oxford University Press (Ages 6 to 8)

My New York, Kathy Jakobesen, Little Brown and Company (Ages 5 and up)

Next Stop Grand Central, Maira Kalman, Putnam Pub Group, New York (Ages 4 to 8)

From the Mixed-Up Files of Mrs. Basil E. Frankweiler, E.L. Konigsburg, Simon Pulse (Ages 9 and up)

Micawber, John Lithgow, Simon and Schuster, New York (Ages 5 to 8)

The Old Pirate of Central Park, Robert Priest, Houghton Mifflin Company, New York (Ages 4 to 8)

This is New York, Miroslav Sasek, Universe Books (Ages 6 and up)

Hey Kid, Want to Buy a Bridge?, Jon Scieszka, Viking, New York (Ages 8 and up)

The Cricket in Times Square, George Selden, Random House, New York (Ages 9 and up)

Eloise, Kay Thompson, Simon and Schuster, New York (Ages 6 and up)

House on East 88th Street, Bernard Waber, Houghton Mifflin Company, New York (Ages 5 to 8)

Lyle, Lyle Crocodile, Bernard Waber, Houghton Mifflin Company, New York (Ages 5 to 8)

You Can't Take a Balloon into the Metropolitan Museum of Art, Jacqueline Preiss Weitzman, Dial Books for Young Readers, New York (Ages 4 and up)

Journey Around New York from A to Z, Marth and Heather Zschock, Commonwealth Editions, Massachusetts (Ages 4 to 8)

Non-Fiction

Brooklyn Bridge, Lynn Curlee, Atheneum Books for Young Readers, New York (Ages 8 and up)

Liberty, Lynn Curlee, Atheneum Books for Young Readers, New York (Ages 8 and up)

The Man Who Walked Between the Towers, Mordicai Gerstein, Millbrook Press (Ages 5 and up)

Under New York, Linda Oatman High, Holiday House, New York (Ages 5 and up)

Empire State Building, Elizabeth Mann, Mikaya Press, New York (Ages 9 and up)

The Brooklyn Bridge, Elizabeth Mann, Mikaya Press, New York (Ages 9 and up)

Storied City: A Children's Guide to New York City, Leonard S. Marcus, Dutton, New York (All ages)

The Inside-Outside Book of New York City, Roxie Munro, Dodd, Mead and Company, New York (Ages 5 and up)

HISTORY TIDBITS

From the get-go, New York City's heart has always beat faster than in other places in the country—and the world. Here are some fun history tidbits:

Downtown Manhattan was the site of the nation's first capital from 1789 until 1790.

Ellis Island embraced more than 12 million immigrants between 1892 and 1954.

The Brooklyn Bridge was the world's longest suspension bridge (as well as the City's tallest structure) when it was built.

The Cathedral Church of St. John the Divine is the world's largest gothic cathedral.

Macy's is the world's largest store, covering 2.1 million square feet of space with more than 500,000 different items.

The oldest municipal golf course, built in 1895, is in Van Cortlandt Park in the Bronx.

The New York Yankees have won more World Series championships (26) than any other Major League Baseball team.

Giovanni da Verrazano is believed to have been the first European to explore the region and Henry Hudson is said to have visited, but it was the Dutch settlements that first began the city of New York. The town of New Amsterdam was established in 1624 on lower Manhattan when the island was bought from Native American inhabitants for $24 worth of trinkets.

In 1664, the city's tallest structure was a two-story windmill. Under the Dutch settlement, Wall Street (yes, there really was a wall here) was the city limit.

The English seized the colony (without firing a shot) in 1664 and renamed it New York City.

The New York Stock Exchange (the world's largest exchange, trading $5.5 trillion annually) started in 1792 when 24 brokers met under a tree in downtown Manhattan. The New York Mercantile Exchange dates to the 1750's when it existed as the Butter and Cheese Exchange.

The first ticker tape parade was in 1886 to celebrate the dedication of the Statue of Liberty. (There have been more than 200 ticker-tape parades in Lower Broadway's Canyon of Heroes.)

NEW YORK CITYPASS

We recommend that you purchase a **New York CityPass**, which gets you into six of the City's most celebrated attractions for one price. The attractions are: The American Museum of Natural History, the Empire State Building Observatory, the Guggenheim Museum, the Museum of Modern Art, the Metropolitan Museum of Art and the Cloisters, and Circle Line Sightseeing Cruises. The booklet also entitles you to a discount on a dinner or brunch cruise on the World Yacht, as well as discounts to Bloomingdale's.

The way it works: Purchase your CityPass booklet at the first of these six attractions you visit (the booklet is sold at each one of them). Bonus: You also avoid most ticket lines. The City Pass booklet is valid for only nine days, beginning the first day you use it. For more information, go to www.citypass.com; you can also purchase tickets online at this website.

Parent Tips

If you are traveling with teens, here are two tips:

• Your teens will love to stay in touch with friends at the CyberCafe, in Times Square.

• If you're in town on a Sunday afternoon, bring your teenager to Blue Smoke/Jazz Standard, a restaurant/club on East 27th between Park and Lexington. Between 1pm and 3pm the downstairs club features jazz by kids for kids. Talented New York City high school jazz musicians perform the jazz. The cover charge is $5, and you can order off a menu—or order nothing at all and just enjoy the music. Bonus: Kids of all ages are allowed in and there's a space for them to dance or burn off energy. Yes, parents are allowed in, too. Note: You'll need to make reservations: Tel. 212/576-2232.

The New York Pass, a "passport" to New York that gives users free entry to more than 40 attractions and discounts at attractions and restaurants is another good money saver. This pass also allows visitors to bypass lines at some attractions. For more information and pricing, call 877/714-1999 or go to www.newyorkpass.com.

TRAVELING WITH YOUR PETS

One of your pet peeves might be that refuse to leave your family's beloved mutt at home. No need to whimper. New York is a pet-friendly town with hotels that welcome pets and there are dog runs in a number of parks. Here are some hotel recommendations for a pet-friendly vacation:

- Tribeca Grand Hotel, 2 Avenue of the Americas, Tel. 877/519-6600, www.tribecagrand.com
- Soho Grand Hotel, 310 West Broadway, 800/965-3000, www.sohogrand.com
- Hotel Gansevoort, 18 Ninth Avenue (at 13th Street), Tel. 877/726-7386, www.hotelgansevoort.com
- Courtyard by Marriott—Manhattan/Times Square South, 114 West 40th Street, Tel. 800/228-9290, www.courtyardtimessquare.com
- Hotel 41, 206 West 41st Street, Tel. 212/703-8600, www.hotel41.com
- Le Parker Meridien Hotel , 118 West 57th Street, Tel. 800/543-4300, www.parkermeridien.com

INDEX

Open Road Publishing

Open Road has launched a radical new concept in travel guides that we call our *Best Of* guides: matching the time you *really* have for your vacation with the right amount of information you need for your perfect trip! No fluff, just the best things to do and see, the best places to stay and eat. Includes one-day, weekend, one-week and two-week trip ideas – in living color! Now what could be more perfect than that?

Best Of Guides

Open Road's Best of Arizona, $14.95
Open Road's Best of The Florida Keys, $14.95
Open Road's Best of Las Vegas, $14.95
Open Road's Best of New York City, $14.95
Open Road's Best of Southern California, $14.95
Open Road's Best of Belize, $14.95
Open Road's Best of Costa Rica, $14.95
Open Road's Best of Honduras, $14.95
Open Road's Best of Panama, $14.95
Open Road's Best of Ireland, $14.95
Open Road's Best of Italy, $16.95
Open Road's Best of Paris, $12.95
Open Road's Best of Provence &
    The French Riviera, $14.95
Open Road's Best of Spain, $14.95

Family Travel Guides

Open Road's Italy with Kids, $16.95
Open Road's Paris with Kids, $16.95
Open Road's Caribbean with Kids, $14.95
Open Road's London with Kids, $14.95
Open Road's New York City with Kids, $14.95
Open Road's Best National Parks With Kids, $12.95
Open Road's Washington, DC with Kids, $14.95
Open Road's Hawaii with Kids, $14.95

Order now at www.openroadguides.com